The Music of

PAUL WINTER

Earth: Voices of a Planet

A Teacher's Guide

Revised Edition
by Marilyn Copeland Davidson

PAUL WINTER

Pioneer of a musical-ecological vision for the past 30 years, Paul Winter has followed a steady course toward his "Earth Music," a celebration of the creatures and cultures of the earth. Also known as "ecological jazz" and "living music," Winter's compositions are uniquely American in the widest sense, being rooted in European and African traditions and interweaving jazz, classical and folk elements with themes from the symphony of nature.

Artist-in-residence at New York's Cathedral of St. John the Divine, Paul Winter has also recorded in the evocative acoustic spaces of wilderness areas such as the Grand Canyon and Siberia's sacred Lake Baikal. "I think that the greatest contribution I could make as a musician would be to encourage people to make their own music," says Winter.

Paul Winter has released 27 recordings and received five Grammy nominations. He won a Grammy award in 1993 for his album, *Spanish Angel*. Honors in recognition for his work for the environment include awards from the World Wildlife Fund, the Humane Society and the United Nations Environment Program.

MARILYN COPELAND DAVIDSON

Marilyn currently teaches in Pequannock, New Jersey. She has presented many workshop sessions across the country, and teaches graduate courses in various colleges and universities. She is Education Consultant for the New Jersey Symphony and past national president of the American Orff-Schulwerk Association. Marilyn is a principal author of *Music and You*, published by Macmillan/McGraw-Hill, and their newest series, *Share the Music*. She is also author of *Melodies from the Far East*, published by Sweet Pipes Inc.

The Music of
PAUL WINTER

EARTH: VOICES OF A PLANET
by Marilyn Copeland Davidson

CONTENTS

Special thanks to Chez Liley for her research and editing assistance on this project.

Editor: Debbie Cavalier
Illustrations: Joann Jane, Hannah Hinchman
Layout: Debbie Johns Lipton
Production Coordinator: Diane Laucirica

TO THE TEACHER: This sequence of lesson suggestions is designed so that a teacher can use all, or any part of it, with one or more classes. The twelve musical selections pay tribute to all seven continents, the oceans, the mountains, and the desert. The selections are:

1. *Appalachian Morning* (Prelude)
2. *Cathedral Forest* (North America)
3. *Call of the Elephant* (Africa)
4. *Antarctica*
5. *Ocean Child* (The Oceans)
6. *Uirapurú Do Amazonas* (South America)
7. *Talkabout* (Australia)
8. *Russian Girls* (Asia)
9. *Black Forest* (Europe)
10. *Song of the Exile*
11. *Under the Sun* (Desert)
12. *And the Earth Spins* (Finale)

Several pages are devoted to each musical selection. The Student Book consists of related activity pages and additional background information for each composition. Emphasis in the Student Book is on providing a variety of opportunities for active individual and group involvement, cooperative learning and higher-level questioning which encourages critical thinking skills. Also included are creative projects in music and cross-curricular connections to other subject areas such as whole language, science, social studies, and so on. Answers appear in Teacher's Guide for reference. They do not appear in the students' book. There are also several pages in this guide which can be used to create overhead projector transparencies.

The first half of the teaching notes for each composition has been developed for use by either a classroom or music teacher, or by both working together. It includes such topics as *Getting to Know the Music, Classroom Extensions* and *Ecological Insights*. The information provided has been carefully researched and is designed to assist the teacher.

The second half, labeled *Musical Discoveries* provides suggestions and material geared toward creating a workable setting for musical improvisation by the student, based on musical understandings gained from listening to each selection of the recording. Although these require musical expertise on the part of the teacher, any of the ideas could also be used by a musically trained classroom teacher. Each selection's teaching notes begins with a brief description of possible Outcome-based Objectives (including suggestion for Portfolio assessments) and ends with a section entitled *FINAL EXPERIENCE*, in which a culminating creative experience is more completely described.

The Student Book is intended to simplify the organization of the students' work and includes a page for each student to keep track of his/her contributions to the class. Alternatively, you may wish to have the students keep a notebook or portfolio of the materials that they use and create as they work with the selections. This collection can serve as a basis for an evaluation of their work.

If time is short, consider having each class listen to all, or most, of the compositions, but creatively develop only one. Then, at some point, the classes could share with each other their assigned compositions and the creative work they have developed in connection with them (art, movement, dramatization, musical improvisation, poetry, and so on). This sharing session could be used as an Earth Day assembly. See page 86 for more ideas on this.

SUGGESTIONS FOR INTRODUCING STUDENTS TO
EARTH: VOICES OF A PLANET

- Have the students find the following on a map of the world (One is included on **Student Book, page #1**): North Pole, South Pole, Equator, Tropic of Cancer, Tropic of Capricorn, the seven continents, the major oceans.
- Tell them that they will be hearing music which represents each of the continents, the ocean, the desert and the mountains.
- Sing the song: *Garden of the Earth* from the recording, *EARTHBEAT* (See page 89 for the music and signing for *Garden of the Earth*. Music and signing for the song are also on **Student page #28.**).

1. APPALACHIAN MORNING (PRELUDE)
by Paul Halley (Back Alley Music, ASCAP)

Outcome Choices:
1. An exhibit of pictures, poems and essays related to the Appalachian Mountains (See below.). This could be tied to a performance event.
2. An Appalachian Rondo: A performance experience, combining descriptive movement, an instrumental improvisation in 5/4 meter, and one or more original free-verse cinquain poems , also with their own original instrumental accompaniment and movement. (Tape the result for portfolios.) (A cinquain is a five line, free verse poem. See directions under Classroom Extensions)

The First Hearing

Before:
Have the students:
- Find the Appalachian mountains on a map of the United States. (**Student page #2**) Discuss features of the area.
- Listen as you tell them the title of the selection. Then, predict what they think the music might sound like.
- Write their predictions on the board (or have them privately write their own predictions).

During:
- Have them test their predictions as to how the music might sound against what they hear.

After:
Have the students:
- Compare their ideas with how the music really sounded.
- Discuss how the music helped them imagine an Appalachian morning.
  (For example: fast tempo, energetic rhythm patterns, sweeping melodies.)

Getting to Know the Music

Have the students:
- Create an informal outline of the composition (See possible example in chart form on page 6). Include details that the students notice about each section. Write their discoveries on the board and have them write them on **Student page #4.**
- Discover the form by assigning a letter to each different melody. Write the form on the board and on their chart on **Student page #4** (Introduction A B C A D B C A Coda).
- Assign a title to each section which is related to the title and subject matter of the composition.
- Draw a picture representing each section.
- Assemble the pictures to show the form. Then, follow the pictures when they hear the music again.

The resulting outline of the composition might look something like the chart shown below. The movement ideas — if they decide to add this — can be developed later, when they are more familiar with the music.

Section Number	Elapsed Time	Theme Used	Musical Features Noted	Possible Title for Section
1 Intro.	(00:00)*	Accompaniment pattern only	Piano solo	Light Dawns
2	(00:05)	First theme [A]	Soprano saxophone, piano. 5/4 meter. Melody is a little like a folk tune.	Sun Appears Over the Mountains
3	(00:27)	First theme repeated [A]	Soprano sax and flute (flute playing melody higher).	(Repeat of above.)
4	(00:50)	Second theme [B]	Soprano sax. 6/4 meter.	Trees Blown by Mountain Breezes
5	(1:15)	Third theme [C]	Section ends with trill. Uses both 6/4 and 5/4 meters in alternating measures.	Birds Fly Overhead
6	(1:45)	First theme again [A]	Melody heard higher. 5/4 meter.	Sun Rises Higher Over the Mountains
7	(2:10)	Fourth theme [D]	Flute and piano. 5/4 meter.	Dark Clouds Form in Front of the Sun
8	(2:27)	Second theme [B]	Soprano sax with flute playing a different part. 5/4 meter.	Sun Reappears, Trees Again Blown
9	(3:02)	Third theme [C]	6/4, 5/4 meters, alternating. Section ends with a trill.	Birds Again Fly Overhead
10	(3:29)	First theme [A]	Soprano saxophone.	Sun Rises Still Higher
11	(4:00)	Ending section (Coda)		Sun's Up!

(TOTAL TIME: 4:15)

* Times shown indicate elapsed time of composition, visible on most CD players. Use these as guidelines in listening for the composition's form. Students often enjoy discovering, or verifying, the exact time that each section starts. This also provides another way for them to develop familiarity with the music — an important step in their developing understanding of - and identity with - the music.

6

- Have small groups write their own statements about the Earth, in the <u>shape</u> of the Earth. You may wish to have them write free-verse poems in the form of a five-line poem called a *cinquain* (*sahn-kahn*) (**Student page #3**).

Guidelines for Writing Cinquains:
The following form is suggested:
Line 1 - The subject (one word).
Line 2 - Two or three words defining the subject.
Line 3 - Three or four words implying movement.
Line 4 - Two or three words conveying or evoking emotions related to the subject.
Line 5 - A one-word synonym for the subject.

Example:

Earth.
Home of all.
Spinning, breathing. Dying?
Help us to save . . .
Life!

- To make their statements or cinquains even more expressive, each group could add a descriptive accompaniment using instruments and/or natural sounds and, if they wish, appropriate movement. Give the groups time to practice their movement and instrumental accompaniments. Then, have them take turns performing for each other.

Move to Show the Form.

Have the students develop movement which shows the form and helps describe each section.

• Divide the class into four groups, each group representing one of the themes.

• Guide them in planning ways to move descriptively during their assigned themes.
  (All can move on the Coda, freezing in place on the last note.)

Listen for Meter and for Rhythm Patterns.

Have the students:

• Make up their own 2- 3- 4- and 5-beat body percussion patterns. For example:

LR	2-Beat Pattern:	Pat L.	Pat R.		
LRR	3-Beat Pattern:	Pat L.	Pat R.	Pat R.	
LRLR	4-Beat Pattern:	Pat L.	Pat R.	Pat L.	Pat R.
LRRLR	5-Beat Pattern:	Pat L.	Pat R.	Pat R.	Pat L.	Pat R.

• Try the different patterns with the A section as they listen to discover that a 5-beat body
  percussion pattern fits best.

• Listen again, trying to do their 5- beat pattern whenever they hear the A theme.

etc.

• Find the section in the music where the melody consists of notes of equal value (The first statement
  of the B theme.).

etc.

Improvise in 5/4 Meter

Have the students find a way to transfer their 5-beat body percussion pattern to D and A on a bass
xylophone, or other low-pitched instrument, and take turns playing it. For example, the 5 beat pattern
above would be played:

For example:

FINAL EXPERIENCE: Create a performance experience. To do so, consider combining descriptive movement for *Appalachian Morning*, the pictures created by the students to show form, an instrumental improvisation in 5/4 meter, and one or more cinquains, each with its own instrumental accompaniment and movement. One possibility might be:

1. Cinquain # 1 - with the planned sounds and movement.

2. Instrumental improvisation in 5/4.

3. *Appalachian Morning*, with the planned movement (using the pictures created by the students).

4. Instrumental improvisation in 5/4.

5. Cinquain #2 - also with planned instrument sounds and movement.

Appalachian Mountains

Name _____ Date _____

Student Page #1: Map of the World

Directions: Fill in each rectangle, correctly labelling the geographic feature to which each is related. Work alone, or in small groups, as directed by the teacher.

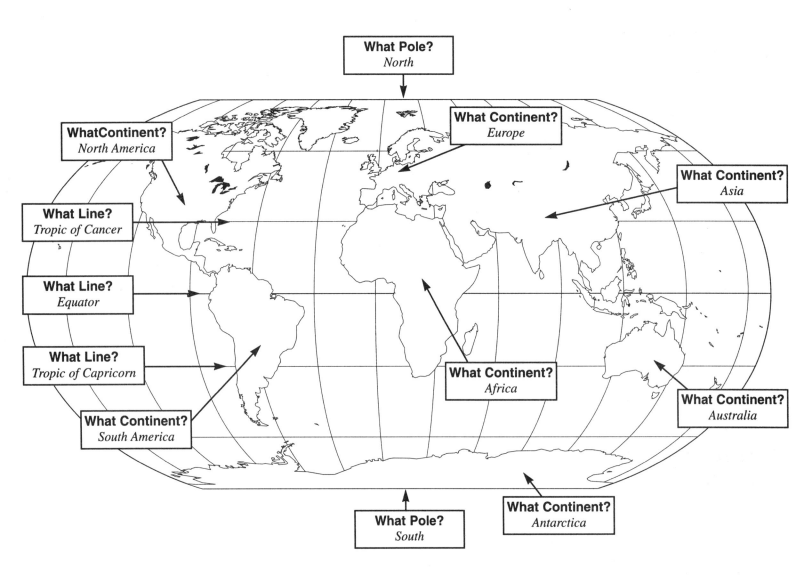

Name _____ Date _____

Student Page #2: Map of the United States

Directions:

1. Fill in each rectangle, correctly labelling the geographic feature to which each is related. Work alone, or in small groups, as directed by the teacher. Do some research as needed.

2. With a group of students, think together about possible questions at the bottom of the page and write your answers.

3. You and your group might wish to gather pictures (photos, drawings, prints) of different scenes of the Appalachian Mountain region and create an exhibit for others to see, with *Appalachian Morning* playing in the background. Include poems and essays you may have written, or art work you have created. Or, you might want to create a multi-media show with transparencies made from some of the pictures you have gathered. The exhibit could be a prelude to performances of your original cinquains, with accompaniment and movement you have created. If you have developed a 5/4 rondo using your cinquains, you could include this in your performance, as well.

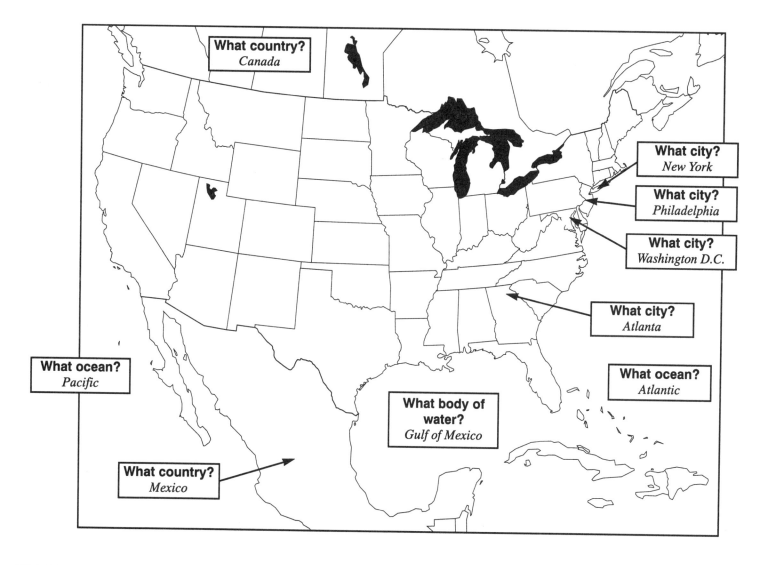

Thinking About The Issues:

Write a possible answer to each of the following questions. Then, talk over your answers with others in the class. More than one answer may have merit.

1. Imagine what the Appalachian Mountain area will be like in fifty years if problems such as acid rain, river pollution and nuclear waste disposal are not solved.
2. Predict what effect this will have on more heavily populated areas of the country.
3. Suggest some solutions for these problems.

Name _____ Date _____

Directions: In small groups, write statements about the Earth. Then, using some or all of these, develop a free-verse poem in the form of a *cinquain (sahnk-ahn)* , a five-line poem. Write the poem in the spaces below, so that it suggests the <u>shape</u> of the Earth. Make your *cinquain* even more expressive by adding a descriptive accompaniment, using instruments and/or natural sounds of your choice. If you wish, appropriate movement can also be developed. Use the space at the bottom of the page to write down your preliminary ideas. Then, work with your group to develop final decisions. After you have practiced your movement and accompaniment, perform your composition for the class.

Line 1 - A 1-word subject: _____

Line 2 - 2 or 3 words
          defining the subject: _____

Line 3 - 3 or 4 words implying,
          or describing,
          movement: _____

Line 4 - 2 or 3 words conveying
          or evoking emotions
          related to the subject: _____

Line 5 - A 1-word synonym
          for the subject: _____

Write your ideas for accompaniment and movement possibilities below.

Line 1:

Line 2:

Line 3:

Line 4:

Line 5:

Name _____ Date _____

Student Page #4: Listening to *Appalachian Morning*

Directions: Listen to *Appalachian Morning*. Work with a group to complete the following:
- Write features of each section that you notice in the space provided below. For example: instruments featured, meter of each section, special effects on instruments.
- Assign a title to each section related to the subject matter of the composition.
- On other paper, draw pictures representing each of the sections.
- Assemble the pictures to show the form. Then, follow the pictures when you hear the music again.

Section Number	Elapsed Time	Theme Used	Features Noted	Possible Title for Section
1 (Introduction)	(00:00)	Accompaniment Pattern Only		
2	(00:05)	First theme [A]		
3	(00:27)	First theme Repeated [A]		
4	(00:50)	Second theme [B]		
5	(1:15)	Third theme [C]		
6	(1:45)	First theme again [A]		
7	(2:10)	Fourth theme [D]		
8	(2:27)	Second theme [B]		
9	(3:02)	Third theme [A]		
10	(3:29)	First theme again [A]		
11	(4:00)	Ending section (*Coda*)		

(TOTAL TIME: 4:15)

2. CATHEDRAL FOREST   (NORTH AMERICA)
by Paul Halley (Back Alley Music, ASCAP)

Outcome Choices: 1. Students "adopt" a nearby tree. Find out all they can about it and how to keep it healthy and take any steps they can to do so. Keep a "photo journal" of the tree through the year.

2. Movement and instrumental improvisations with showing of transparencies of trees and owls. (Videotape the result for portfolios.)

| The First Hearing |

Before:
- Have the students imagine the interior of a great cathedral. Then, ask them to think of ways that a forest might suggest a cathedral to some observers. (For example: Tall trees with branches arching overhead might suggest the vaulted roof of a cathedral. The quiet, awe-inspiring stillness of the forest could be reminiscent of the atmosphere in a great cathedral.)
- Tell the class the title of the composition they are about to hear and discuss its meaning.
- Read to the class the comments for this selection from the booklet included with the recording.
- If possible, show the students pictures of redwood or any old growth forests.

During:
Have the students:
- Imagine walking through a forest. Think about what in the music suggests such a walk. (For example: the drum sets a somber mood, the upward-moving melody suggests the soaring height of the trees, the steady tempo might suggest a leisurely walking speed.)
- Listen for the sound of the spotted owl.
- Listen for the different qualities of sounds on the drum and try to identify the type of drum being used. (It is a frame drum, similar to what many students may know as a hand drum. It has a large head and a narrow frame and is usually played without a mallet, as is the case in this recording. Similar styles of frame drums are found in many cultures all over the world.)

After:
Have the students
- Discuss what they heard in the music — its effect on their feelings and emotions. (Answers will vary. Accept all thoughtful ones.)
- Decide what in the music seemed to create its mood. (For example: The upward moving melody suggests the sweeping height of the tall trees and the owl's flight; the call of the owl is heard several times during the selection; the tone quality of the different drumming sounds adds to the somber mood of the music.)

Getting to Know the Music

Have the students:

- Explore different ways of creating sounds on a drum (Using the heel of the hand, using the thumb, using the finger tips, drumming with fingers for rapid repetitions, snapping fingers near the head of the drum so that it is tapped by one finger, rubbing the drum head with a moistened thumb, deadening the sound immediately, and so on).
- Listen for, and to try to identify, some of the different drumming techniques used in the composition. Then, try some of the techniques themselves.
- Listen to the melody in the first section of the composition and decide if it moves mostly by steps or by skips. (It moves mostly by steps. A step is from one tone to a scale tone. A skip is from one tone to a scale tone two or more steps away.)

Classroom Extensions

Have the students:

1. Make a round frame drum. (See Page 22)
2. Read about spotted owls. Discuss.
3. Read Owl Moon, by Jane Yolen. Scholastic Inc., New York, 1987. (Younger students will enjoy having the book read to them as *Cathedral Forest* is played. Older students might read it to younger ones as part of a presentation on saving owls and forests.)
4. Find out about threatened trees and birds in their own area. Share their findings with the class.
5. "Adopt" a nearby tree. Find out all they can about it and how to keep it healthy and take any steps they can to do so. Keep a "photo journal" of the tree through the year. (**Student page #6**)
6. Do research on why we need forests. (See Ecological Insights below.) Share research with the class.

Ecological Insights

Spotted Owl

The northern spotted owl is about 17 inches high with a wingspan of 43 inches, weighs just over a pound, and must eat that weight in quarry daily. It is strictly nocturnal and depends on large areas of old growth forest. The spotted owl's population is decreasing because of habitat loss. The Forest Service uses it as an "indicator species" in the Pacific Northwest. Its presence implies a habitat is appropriate for other species that have similar requirements.

Old Growth Forests

Forests are complex ecosystems. They contain numerous plant species and are a vital habitat for the many animals which depend on them for food and shelter. In a process called photosynthesis, with the aid of chlorophyll as a catalyst, trees combine carbon dioxide from the atmosphere with other nutrients to make food for growth. Collectively, trees hold huge stores of carbon dioxide. They absorb the impact of rains, filter streams, hold back the floods and preserve the springs. They help create fertile soils and protect from erosion. They supply oxygen and humidity and are the source of many useful products.

Tree Species in the Old Growth Forest

In the north: mixed spruce and hemlock, and dense clusters of giant Sitka spruce along the rivers; spruce and Douglas fir along the Cascades of British Columbia, Washington and Oregon. In the south: redwood forests, forests of mixed fir and pockets of broad-leaf forests.

The sitka spruce (Picea sitchensis) grows to 180 - 200 feet. Its sharp-pointed needles are bright blue-green above and blue-white beneath. It likes to grow where the summers are damp and cool.

The Douglas fir has thick, dark foliage. It can grow to 200 feet and has a distinctive craggy, cracked bark.

The coast redwood (Sequoia sempervirens) of California and Oregon is the world's largest tree, and can grow to 350 feet.

Resources:
David Kelly and Gary Braasch, Secrets of the Old Growth (Salt Lake City: Gibbs Smith, 1988)
<u>Organizations concerned with old growth forests</u>
Siskiyou Regional Education Project, P.O. Box 220, Cave Junction, OR 97523
Headquarters, P.O. Box 729, Ashland, OR 97520
Save America's Forests, 4 Library Court, S.E., Washington DC 20003
Native Forest Council, P.O. Box 2171, Eugene, OR 97402

Spotted Owl

Develop Familiarity with the Form. (Student page #7)
• Have the students listen and figure out the form (Introduction ABA Coda,) and write it on the board. Then, form groups and have the class listen again, indicating with raised hands the beginning of each section. Have one person in each group watch the time elapsed read-out on the compact disc player or on a clock, and note the exact time that each section begins. Have the class listen again to note any other details of each section ((Instruments Used, Dynamic Effects, Rhythm Features) as one or two in each group make notes on movement or dramatization possibilities. Add these to their outlines.

For example:

Section Number	Elapsed Time	Theme Used Features)	Features Noted (Instruments Used, Dynamic Effects, Rhythm Features)	Possible Movement Ideas for Section
1 (Intro-duction)	00:00	Introduction	Frame drum, spotted owl, piano, drum	
2	00:23	[A]	Flute begins, saxophone plays on repeat	
3	1:45	Interlude	Crescendo, upward movement; then, decrescendo leading into next section	
4	2:18	[B]	Saxophone and cello play new melody; piano plays repeated sixteenth-note patterns. Shaker added. Flute joins melody on repeat. Later, flute solo with cymbal and drums added. Then saxophone re-enters.	
5	4:14	[A]	A Section returns — louder this time	
6	4:51	Coda	At 5:23 spotted owl, piano, drum are heard, as at beginning	

TOTAL TIME: 5:49

Discover and Practice the Meter.

Have the students:

- Figure out the meter (slow 3/4) by patting gently on each downbeat (beat one) and counting the beats to themselves.
- Step only on the downbeat, imagining that they are walking through the forest, viewing the trees and looking for the spotted owl.
- Develop one or more patterns in 3/4 meter that they can pat or play on one or more unpitched instruments along with the recording.

For example:

Drum $\frac{3}{4}$ ‖: ♩ 𝄽 𝄽 | 𝄽 ♩ ♩ :‖

Log Drum $\frac{3}{4}$ ‖: 𝄽 ♫♩ | ♩ 𝄽 𝄽 :‖

(Try for a different tone color for each individual sound by using different drum techniques and by playing different places on the log drum for each note in the part. If a log drum is not available, you can use alternate sound sources, such as: several wood blocks of varying sizes and/or density, temple blocks, student desks, floor, and so on.)

Create Expressive Movement

Have the students:

- Move in slow motion to express the mood of the music. (Encourage them to begin a new motion with the down beat of each phrase, then continue that motion through the phrase. They can move individually, mirror a partner face-to-face, or "shadow" a partner - with the leader turned away from the follower.)
- Develop a movement/dramatization in which one or more students depict moving through a forest as the rest freeze in shapes which suggest the character of the great trees of the forest. One or more students could portray the spotted owl.

Create Instrumental Improvisations

Have the students:

- Develop drum improvisations in a slow 3/4 meter (about ♩ = 60) over a repeated low E on bass xylophone or other low-register instrument. (Encourage them to try different playing techniques on the drum.)
- Add melodic improvisation in E natural minor (E F# G A B C D E') or E *la* pentatonic (E GAB DE') on recorder, metallophone, or other pitched instrument.
- Use the form of the composition as a basis for improvisation. For example:

Introduction: Drums and/or other percussion alone, over bass xylophone, playing a repeated E on the beat. (These instruments continue throughout.)

A Section:	Recorder improvises.
Interlude:	Drums and/or other percussion alone.
B Section:	Metallophone improvises.
A Section:	Recorder improvises.
Coda:	Drums and/or other percussion alone.

(Students should decide on the length of each section and how they will know when each new section is to begin.)

- Create overhead transparencies of trees and owls and display them in a partially darkened room during the improvisation.

FINAL EXPERIENCE: Combine the movement and instrumental improvisations with the transparencies of trees and owls, as described above.

(Permission to photocopy pages 19 - 21)

How to Make a Round Frame Drum with
Handle and Beater
by Craig Woodson, Ph.D.

Materials

1. Cardboard tube, 8-inch diameter, 1/8-inch wall thickness (or more), 3 inches deep
   (Called concrete form tube, bought at building supply stores)
2. Strapping tape, 3/4-inch wide, approximately 6 feet. (This tape is plastic with strings in it.)
3. Wooden embroidery hoops, inner solid ring, outer broken ring with screw to tighten, 9-inch diameter.
4. Plastic bag in cereal or cracker boxes that holds contents. Don't use paper bag.
5. Dowel stick, 3/8-inch diameter, 9 inches long, cut from longer piece with serrated knife.
6. Paper towel or paper napkin. (one sheet)

Tools

1. Serrated kitchen knife
2. Ruler, 6-inch or 12-inch
3. Pencil

How to Make

The Drum Frame

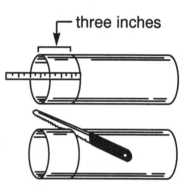

1. Mark 3-inch length on one end of the tube with the ruler and pencil by dragging the ruler and pencil around the tube as you go.

2. Cut the tube on the mark with the serrated knife, using any of the following: forward motion only, backward motion only, forward and backward motion, or by punching through with the knife's tip then sawing back and forth.

The Drumhead

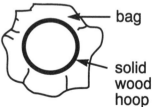

3. Take the hoops completely apart and lay the opened plastic bag on the solid hoop. Then press the broken hoop over the plastic as intended for embroidery work. Gradually pull the plastic as the tension screw is tightened so that there are no wrinkles in the drumhead area. Finally, cut off the excess around the hoop as shown. (or see note)

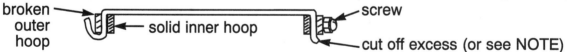

NOTE: You have the option of taping the excess plastic around the outer hoop.

Tensioning the Drumhead

4. Place the drumhead on the frame with the hoops facing down as shown.

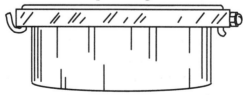

5. Begin tightening the drumhead by sticking one end of the strapping tape to the head as shown and pulling the tape over the hoops, down side of the frame, under the frame to the other side, then sticking it on the opposite side to the frame. (Not touching the head)

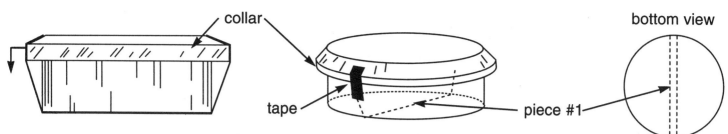

collar

tape

piece #1

bottom view

All the tape pieces will have to be tightened with considerable force in order to bring the head up to tension. As it pulls down, the drumhead will form a "collar" or slight drop or bevel from the mouth. This shows that the drumhead is tightening.

6. With the same technique, a second piece of strapping tape should be pulled across 90 degrees from the first piece in an opposing diameter as shown.

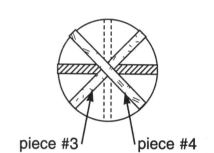

bottom view

piece #1

piece #2

7. Again, with the same technique, two more pieces should be put on to further tighten the drumhead as shown (45 degrees from the first and second pieces). This should completely tighten the head. If wrinkles appear there will be a buzzing sound when the head is struck. It will sound somewhat like a snare drum. It is difficult to reposition the strapping tape without denting the drumhead bag material, so take care to position it correctly the first time.

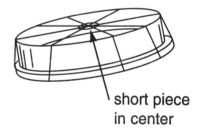

piece #3   piece #4

The Handle

8. The drum is held at the center of the taped piece in the bottom of the frame. The sticky part can be stuck together to avoid sticking to the hand. Also, a short 3-inch piece should be wrapped around the center to unify the handle and further tighten the system.

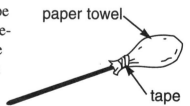

bottom view

short piece in center

The Beater

9. The beater should be prepared by wrapping one end with scraps of strapping tape or by random twists of tape to about the size of a large elongated marble. To prevent dimpling on the head, a piece of paper towel should be wrapped around the beater end and taped on as shown. NOTE: The drum should not be struck with the wooden end of the beater as this will dimple or break the head.

paper towel

tape

Playing Technique

10. The drum can be played with the hand or with the beater or with either in combination. Care should be taken not to hit the drumhead too hard as this will dimple the head and make it buzz. If the buzz is desired for a special effect, be careful not to dimple the head too much as this might break the head. By squeezing the handle area under the head the pitch of the drum can be raised. Holding it more loosely will cause the pitch to be lowered.

(Permission to photocopy)

23

Name _____ Date _____

Student Page #5: Forests of the Northwestern United States Area

Directions: Find out more about the forests of the Northwest United States. With a group of students, think together about possible answers for the following questions. Write a possible answer to each of the following questions in the space provided. Then, talk over your answers with others in the class. More than one answer may have merit.

Thinking About The Issues

1. Write down, then discuss, the main points of view in the conflict in the Northwestern United States between loggers needing to cut down trees to earn a living and environmentalists trying to save the forests and the habitats of animal life, such as the spotted owl.

2. Formulate a possible compromise solution to this problem. Decide who would need to implement such a solution. Discuss your answers with your group.

3. Decide what action would need to be taken to implement your solution. Plan and share a dramatic presentation that would convince others to support your solution. Use the music, *Cathedral Forest*, and your own improvisations as part of your presentation.

Name _____ Date _____

Student Page #6: A Photo Journal of An "Adopted" Tree

Directions:
1. "Adopt" a nearby tree.
2. Find out all you can about it and how to keep it healthy. Take any steps you can to do so.
3. Keep a "photo journal" of the tree through rest of the school year. You may wish to use this page to mount your first picture. Add additional pages as necessary. Under each picture that you later add, put the date and any comments about the condition of the tree that you feel are important.

"Adopted Tree" Description

Location of "adopted" tree: _____

Tree Type (Genus): _____

Notable characteristics or functions of this tree:

_____

_____

Reasons for my selecting this tree:

_____

_____

Ways to keep this tree healthy:

_____

_____

Picture of tree at time of "adoption:"

Description of tree's condition
at time of "adoption:"

Name _____ Date _____

Student Page #7: Form, Musical Features and Possible Movement for
Cathedral Forest

Directions:

1. Develop familiarity with the music and its form by following the chart below as you listen in small groups. One person should check the elapsed time shown for the beginning of each section on the compact disc player or on a clock. Later, after exploring the various possibilities, write down ideas for movement or dramatization. Others should note any other details of each section. Compare ideas after listening and add as appropriate to your outline.

Section Number	Elapsed Time	Theme Used	Features Noted (Instruments Used, Dynamic Effects, Rhythm Features)	Possible Movement Ideas for Section
1 (Intro-duction)	00:00	Introduction		
2	00:23	[A]		
3	1:45	Interlude		
4	2:18	[B]		
5	4:14	[A]		
6	4:51	Coda		

(TOTAL TIME: 5:49)

3. Call of the Elephant (AFRICA)
by Paul Berliner, Kwaku Dadey, Paul Halley, Paul Winter (Bar-Loma Music, ASCAP; Living Earth Music, BMI)

Outcome Choices:
1. Poems or essays on elephants and/or other endangered animals.
2. Improvisations and original poems or essays used as introductions for dramatizations created to perform with the recording of *Call of the Elephant.* (Tape the results for portfolios.)
3. An improvisation, created in cooperative groups, using the dynamic plan of *Call of the Elephant.* (Tape the result for portfolios.)

The First Hearing

Before:
- Have the students find Africa on the map.
- Read part or all of the information in the booklet accompanying the recording, including instruments used.
- Play the music for the students.
- Use an elephant silhouette on an overhead projector to dramatize the students' initial contact with the music. (Use your own drawing, or Page 31, Elephant Silhouette.) Dim the lights in the classroom and, as the music begins, project the silhouette for the class to view as they listen. For a larger, more effective image, project it directly onto a sheet, with the overhead projector behind it, turned toward the class (See below.). To avoid light shining in eyes of the class, put the projector on the floor and tilt it upward.

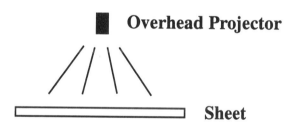

During:
- Ask the students to try to visualize the scene suggested by the music (with elephants grazing on an African veldt).

After:
- Have the students decide on the over-all mood of the music (serious, sad, somber) then, speculate on the reason for this (the plight of the endangered elephants). Ask them to think about this when they listen to the music again.

Getting to Know the Music

Have the students listen to the music, then write a general description of each section of the composition, including the time that each section begins.
For example:

0:00 Elephant sounds.
0:34 Free rhythm - elephant sounds alternating with kudu horn, alto saxophone, and Ghanaian drum. Cello enters.
2:49 Music becomes more and more rhythmic as piano, bass, foot bells, and guitar enter.
3:54 Soprano saxophone plays the main melody.
5:10 Elephant sounds, kudu horn, alto saxophone (like the opening).
TOTAL TIME: 6:50

Classroom Extensions

Have the students:
- Find out more about this environmental issue. Read about elephants and the survival of the African veldt. Find out about the living habits of elephants (such as: where they normally live, what they eat, how they raise their young, if they prefer to live alone or with others in a group, whether or not they are nocturnal, how long they live, how they communicate).
- Write poems or essays about elephants.
- Visit a local zoo to study elephants.
- Find out about the hunting of elephants and sale of ivory and products that use ivory.
- Find out about endangered animals in their own area. If possible, collect taped sounds of these animals.

Ecological Insights

Elephants
Katharine Payne, whose work with humpback whales in the 1960's, revealed extraordinary findings concerning their songs, also discovered that elephants were the first land mammals known to use low-frequency sounds. (Ms. Payne spent the last ten years studying elephants in Africa. She is based at the Cornell Laboratory of Ornithology, near Ithaca, New York). Elephant calls are usually at frequencies of 14 to 35 hertz, (Human hearing starts at about 30 hertz). Such low frequencies are able to penetrate long distances. It is thought that elephants use sound to space themselves within a group. Individuals of a family that are visually separated, perhaps over several miles, can coordinate their movements and warn each other of danger. Females live in independent family groups often miles away from the males, but have a rumbling love song to communicate when they go into heat.

Suggested resources:
Jane E. Brody, "Picking up Mammals' Deep Notes", The New York Times, 9 November, 1993
Heathcote Williams, Sacred Elephant (Westminster, Maryland: Crown Publishers, Inc., 1989)

Musical **D**iscoveries

Listen for Definite and Indefinite Beat

• Ask the students to listen to the music and focus on the rhythms. Help them to become aware of the difference in rhythmic effect between the opening and closing sections, which have no definite beat, and the rhythmic middle section.

• Have them decide what these rhythmic differences might suggest.
(For example: the sections with free rhythms could be depicting the view over the vast African scene and the free movements of the elephants' bodies as they swing their trunks, perhaps spraying them selves with water, or reaching up to pull leaves off a tree as they feed. The more rhythmic section could depict the movement of the elephants as they go to a different place.)

Listen for Tone Color

Help the students recognize as many of the instruments as they can. The instruments heard are: a drum (from Ghana), alto saxophone, soprano saxophone, kudu horn (made from a horn of a kudu, a kind of antelope. See illustration, below.), piano, bass, foot bells (jingles strapped around one foot and played by tapping one's foot on the ground), and guitar.

A Kudu

Compare the low elephant sound with the other instruments heard on the recording...
Kudu Horn, etc.

Have the students:

• Recognize the contrasting pitch levels between the low elephant sounds and the higher sounds of the kudu horn and the soprano saxophone.

• Find the lowest pitched sound available in the classroom and compare it with the sound of the elephant heard on the recording. For example, the lowest note on the piano is 27.5 cycles (or vibrations) per second, while the sound of the elephant heard on the recording is 14-35 cycles per second.

• Think of a high-pitched sound that elephants make (the characteristic sound of the elephant trumpeting). Play a recording of this sound, if available, for purposes of comparison.

Recognize Dynamic Changes (Student page #9, Part A)

Guide the students to become aware of the changes in dynamics in the music (soft at the beginning, the *crescendo*, during which the dynamic level gradually increases, the *decrescendo* at the end, which returns to the soft dynamic level of the opening).

Create A Dramatization (Student page #9, Part A)

Have the students plan a dramatization to perform with the music. First, have them decide a specific thing that each instrument and natural sound represents (kudu horn, saxophones, drum, cello, and, of course, the elephant sound), who will portray each sound, and how they might do so. Then, with the music, the students move only when they hear their assigned sound in the composition. They should also decide what the dynamic changes might represent (For example: The decrescendo could suggest the elephants going off into the distance.) and act this out to bring their dramatization to an end.

Develop an Improvisation (Student page #9, Part B)

Encourage the students, working in small groups of three to five, to create their own improvisations using drum, recorder (and/or other instruments of their choice), and taped animal sounds they may have collected (local endangered and non-endangered species, pets, zoo animals, commercial sound effect records, sounds from television programs, wild animals — such as squirrels and birds, and so on). They may use any available instruments or sound sources of their choice, and they are free to use whatever rhythms or pitch combinations they think are appropriate. However, they are to use the basic form of *Call of the Elephant* as a frame-work for the improvisation.

For example:

• Begin with the taped animal sounds.

• Improvise on instruments in a free rhythm with no definite beat.

• Have each instrument gradually begin to move into a definite repeated pattern for a short period of time.

• Have each instrument, one by one, return to the free rhythm.

• End with a decrescendo, and a return of the animal sound.

FINAL EXPERIENCE: Have the students use their improvisations, and some of their original poems or essays, as an introduction for the dramatization which they created to perform with the recording of *Call of the Elephant*, or combine their own improvisation with the dramatization.

(Permission to photocopy)

Name _____ Date _____

Directions: Fill in each rectangle, correctly labelling the geographic feature to which each is related. Work alone, or in small groups, as directed by the teacher.

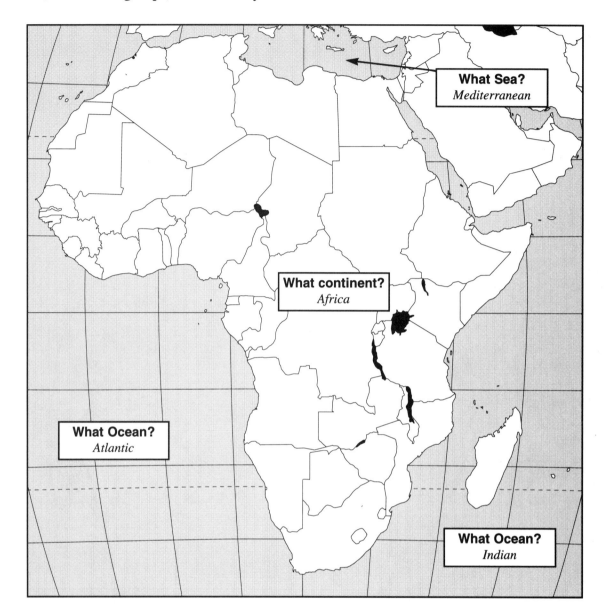

What Sea?
Mediterranean

What continent?
Africa

What Ocean?
Atlantic

What Ocean?
Indian

Thinking About The Issues:

1. Research and discuss, the hunting of elephants, the sale of ivory and products that use ivory.

2. What endangered animals are in your own area?

3. If possible, collect taped sounds of these animals.

4. Formulate possible ideas to help save these animals.

Name _____ Date _____

Student Page #9: *A Dramatization and Improvisation (Part A)*

Directions:

1. Listen for the dynamic changes (Changes in volume) in *Call of the Elephant*. Plot the dynamic changes here in any design that does not use words. Discuss your ideas and compare them with others in the class.

2. Plan movement/dramatization to perform with the music. First, decide what each sound represents, who will portray each sound, and general guidelines as to how this might be done. (With the music, students are to move only when they hear their assigned sound.)

SOUND	What each sound represents	Who will portray each sound	General guidelines for each movement.
kudu horn			
saxophones			
drum			
cello			
elephant sound			

3. Decide what the dynamic changes might represent and how to show this in your dramatization. Write your answer here.

Name _____ Date _____

Student Page #9: *A Dramatization and Improvisation (Part B)*

Directions:

4. Develop an improvisation. Working in small groups of three to five, create your own improvisations using drum, recorder (and/or other instruments of your choice), and taped animal sounds you may have collected (local endangered and non-endangered species, pets, zoo animals, commercial sound effect records, sounds from television programs, wild animals — such as squirrels and birds, and so on). Use any available instruments or sound sources of your choice. You are free to use whatever rhythms or pitch combinations you think are appropriate. However, you are to use the basic form and dynamic plan of *Call of the Elephant* as a framework for the improvisation.

For example:
- Begin with the taped animal sounds.
- Improvise on instruments in a free rhythm with no definite beat.
- Have each instrument gradually begin to move into a definite repeated pattern for a short period of time.
- Have each instrument, one by one, return to the free rhythm.
- End with a *decrescendo*, and a return of the animal sound.

Use the space below to write down the plan for your improvisation.

Animal sounds to be used at the beginning and end and name of group member responsible for this effect:

Instruments and players at the beginning (section without a definite beat):

Order in which instruments will begin to improvise within a steady beat (Reverse this order for the return to free rhythm and *decrescendo*.)

34

4. ANTARCTICA
by Paul Halley, Paul Winter (Back Alley Music, ASCAP; Living Earth Music, BMI)

Outcome Choices: 1. Poems about extreme cold and/or wind, using descriptive words to make the listener "feel" these conditions.
2. Students combine their wind movements and wind instrumental improvisations with their poems and "ice music" to create their own Antarctica composition. (Tape the result for portfolios.)

The First Hearing

Before:
• Read to the students all or part of the information in the booklet included with the recording. Invite them to imagine what the Antarctic, cold and wind feel like.

During:
• Ask the students to listen for wind sounds and the sounds of the Weddell seals (The seals are heard at approximately 4:00 of elapsed time). Have them try to identify the instruments that they hear on the recording (pipe organ and soprano saxophone).

After:
• Have the students relate what they heard as they listened to the music (the wind, the seals, the instruments).
• Describe characteristics of the music that suggest the cold and the vastness of Antarctica, (no meter; long sustained sounds; no definite ending; very few instruments used, suggesting the lack of great variety in what the eye sees, as compared to other areas of the Earth; and the use of instruments which require wind to create their sound [such as the pipe organ and the soprano saxophone]).

Getting to Know the Music

In order to help the students become more familiar with the music, have them listen again and make a list of the sounds, in the order in which each begins and stops. Then, have them listen once more and write down the exact time that each instrument or other sound begins and stops. One student can monitor the time and write it on the board for the rest to copy into their notes. The result will look like this:

0:00   Wind sound begins.
0:28   Pipe organ begins.
0:35   Pipe organ melody begins.
1:44   Soprano saxophone begins.
3:59   Seals are heard.
4:03   Seals stop.
4:58   Saxophone stops.
5:05   Organ stops (Only the wind is heard to the end.).
5:20   Wind stops.
TOTAL TIME: 5:20

Help the students to realize that the over-all dynamic effect of the composition is a long *crescendo* (gradual increase in the volume) up to when the seals are heard, followed by a long *decrescendo* (gradual decrease in volume) to the end.

Have the students:

• Write poems about extreme cold and/or wind, using descriptive words to make the listener "feel" these conditions.

• Find out more about protecting Antarctica, regarding the danger from the hole in the ozone layer and its possible effect on our climate and general well-being.

• Research the 1961 Antarctica Treaty, in which countries agreed that Antarctica should " be used exclusively for peaceful purposes." What countries signed it? It was subject to review in 1991. Was it reviewed? What happened? Has the easing of tensions between the United States and the former U.S.S.R. resulted in any cooperative scientific research in the area?

• Think about the different names and voices of the ice and how these names might have come about. (These are mentioned in the booklet included with the recording.) (**Student page #11, Part A: *Ice Music*.**) Bring some ice into the classroom and listen to the sounds it makes as you break it up into pieces. Then, imagine the sounds that each type of ice might make and try to re-create these imagined sounds with available percussion instruments (cabasa, maracas, guiro, and so on) or other sound sources to create "ice music." For example:

    Green "growler" (Appears as green. Makes growling sounds - One or more cabasas, ratchets or guiros played with long, grinding sounds.

    New "frazil" fibrous (Newly formed and fibrous. Makes a rasping sound.) - Maracas played with light, short repeated sounds.

    "Pancake" ice, rubbed round - Play hand drums by rubbing the heads with a circular motion.

    "Drift" ice, which disintegrated, turns to "brash" - ratchets played to suggest disintegrating ice.

• Listen to the poems written by class members. Select several to prepare for an in-class performance. Form small groups, one for each poem. Each group is to use their own improvised "ice music" (described above) to accompany one of the selected poems. (Give the groups adequate time for preparation and rehearsal. Then, have each group perform its poem with its sound setting.)

• Research the Weddell seals and how they survive in the extreme cold of Antarctica.

• Find out about other animal life in Antarctica (for example, penguins).

Antarctica
Antarctica is a continent of wind and regenerating forces. The physical, chemical and biological processes occurring in the ocean affect the whole planet.

In the early 1770's, the Englishman James Cook became the first to cross the Antarctic Circle and sail as far as 70° S. In the 1800's, further exploration was carried out by whalers and seal-hunters in search of prey. In the season of 1820 - 1821, James Weddell, a Scot and captain of the sealing ship Jane, was exploring and charting the islands around the South Shetlands. One of his men reported meeting a mermaid who had a reddish face and long green hair. After staring at the sailor for several minutes, the mermaid made a "musical noise" and disappeared. Weddell managed to catch one, which turned out to be a seal, later named after him.

The Weddell Seal (Leponychotes weddlli) lives at the edge of the ice pack and spends most of its time below the ice. Its specially shaped incisors enable it to rasp open breathing holes. The Weddell is one of the largest seals and can probably dive the deepest. During a dive, its heart rate slows to a quarter its normal speed, enabling it to reach depths of 300m or 400m (approximately 1,000 - 1,300 feet) where the Antarctic cod, its main food source, is plentiful. Its deepest recorded dive is 600m, and its longest recorded dive lasted 73 minutes.

Ice:
Explorers of Antarctica found it very important to differentiate between the various kinds of ice they encountered.

Each year part of the Southern Ocean ices over after a gradual process of freeze, thaw, and re-freeze. Waves coalesce the ice fibers of the first thin freeze into tiny platelets of ice called **"frazil"**, that float on the surface, easily cut through by the ice-breaker ships. The **"frazil"** joins into larger round plates with raised edges that are called **"pancakes."** Strong winds soon push them to shore where they disintegrate to slush until increasing cold fuses them into **"pack."**

Most of the **"pack"** ice melts during its first summer. **"Drift"** ice forms when a solid pack of ice fragments into **"brash"** (small bits of ice debris). **"Growlers"** are small pieces of green ice, scarcely visible above the surface of the water. Their ominous name reflects the threat they pose to smaller ships, and comes from the noise they make grating along a boat's hull.

Background to the Antarctica Treaty
What little ice-free and snow-free land there is to be found on Antarctica is mostly found on the Peninsula. The thinly dispersed community of animals and plants that resides there is very vulnerable to disruption. It is this level, ice-free terrain that is usually chosen for the construction of field stations (68 Antarctic bases have been occupied). The effects of construction and other human activities include the introduction of exotic species (such as rats!), pollution, and disturbance from traffic and tourism. Valuable deposits of metals and fossil fuels have either been identified, or are thought to exist in Antarctica. The United Kingdom, Argentina, Chile, New Zealand, Australia, France and Norway are nations laying territorial claim on Antarctica and its related islands. Other nations that have made explorations in the Antarctic include Japan, Brazil, China, South Africa, West Germany, Belgium; also the United States and Russia, both of which have refused to claim territory or recognize the claims of the countries.

Resources:
Sanford Moss, *A Natural History of the Antarctic Peninsula*, illustrations by Lucia deLeiris (New York: Columbia University Press, 1988)

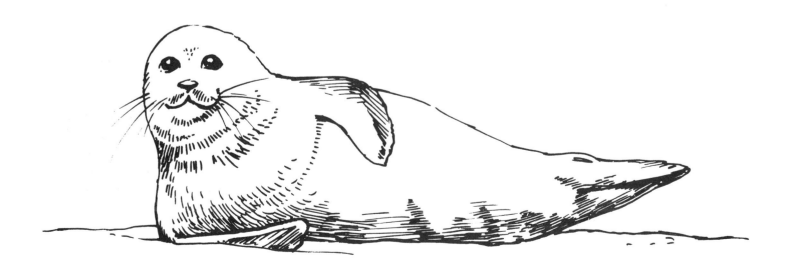

Improvise Descriptive Movement and Music

Have the students:

• Imagine <u>being</u> the wind. Create sounds that suggest wind sounds. Then, take turns trying to move as the wind moves. Move to their own wind sounds. Suggestions: Use silver streamers. These can be purchased or can be made of aluminum foil.

• Listen to *Antarctica*, moving like the wind when they hear the sounds of the wind.

• Find ways to create music on classroom instruments that suggests the sound of the wind.

• Create an improvised composition suggesting the wind, using the *crescendo/decrescendo* effect similar to that in *Antarctica*.

• Combine the movement with improvised "Ice Music." (**Student page #11, Part B:** *Ice Music.*)

Learn About Pipe Organs

Have the students read and discuss the following page: ***About Pipe Organs.***

• Take a field trip to see a pipe organ. Visit the loft where the pipes are housed. Talk to the organist. Listen to the instrument being played. Learn about the organ and how it is played: the various stops and how they work, the reasons why there are several keyboards (manuals), how the foot pedals are played, the reason for the different lengths of the pipes, the varying tone colors of the different ranks of pipes (strings, diapason, reeds, trumpets, and so on), and how *crescendi* and *decrescendi* are produced, when pipe organs were invented, and so on. Compare the sound of a pipe organ with that of an electronic organ.

FINAL EXPERIENCE: Have the students combine their wind movements and wind instrumental improvisations with their poems and "ice music" to create their own Antarctica composition.

About Pipe Organs

St. John the Divine Cathedral in New York City

The organ heard on the recording is at St. John the Divine in New York City. This Cathedral is the largest Protestant church in the world and is home to the Episcopal Bishop of New York.

The great organ at St. John the Divine Cathedral

The instrument was built in 1910 by Ernest M. Skinner and Robert Hope Jones. Electric power, still relatively new, was used to control the valves of the pipes, the expression boxes (which permit the organist to create gradual changes in dynamics), and the wind chests where the pipes are located. The organ utilizes an early type of computer which memorized pre-selected combinations of stops.

The Cathedral is still not completely finished. Work on it has been going on almost continuously throughout this century. By 1941, the Cathedral had reached its full length of 601 feet. At that time, extensive changes in the organ were necessary. In 1954, the organ was rebuilt into the instrument it is today by G. Donald Harrison of the Aeolian-Skinner Organ Company, with assistance from Joseph Whiteford. Although many changes have been made on this organ, a large part of the original instrument is still intact.

With 8,035 pipes, this is one of the most complete and versatile organs in existence. Randy Gilberti, the curator of the Great Organ, who maintains the instrument, says: "I wish more people would come up to the pipe chamber. They could see how incredible the organ is from the inside. A photograph will never capture the magnificence and beauty." (Permission to photocopy)

Name _____ Date _____

Student Page #10: *Map of Antarctica*

Directions: Fill in each rectangle, correctly labelling the geographic feature to which each is related. Work alone, or in small groups, as directed by the teacher.

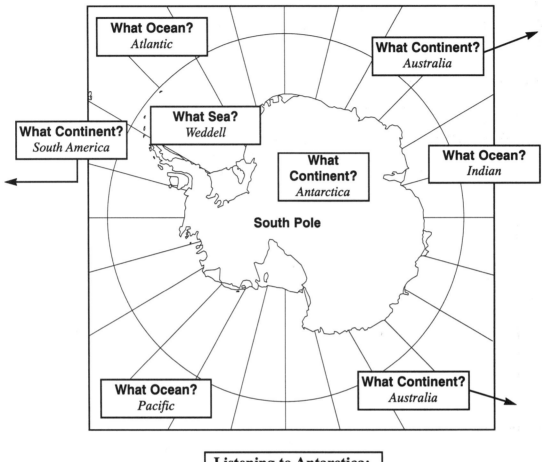

| **Listening to Antarctica:** |

1. Listen to *Antarctica* and list the sounds you hear. Write down the exact time that each starts and stops. One student can monitor the time on a stop watch, clock, or digital timer on the CD player, then write it on the board for the rest of the class to copy into their notes.

> *0:00   Wind sound begins.*
> *0:28   Pipe organ begins.*
> *0:35   Pipe organ melody begins.*
> *1:44   Soprano saxophone begins.*
> *3:59   Seals are heard.*
> *4:03   Seals stop.*
> *4:58   Saxophone stops.*
> *5:05   Organ stops (Only the wind is heard to the end.).*
> *5:20   Wind stops.*
> *TOTAL TIME: 5:20*

2. As you listen, plot the dynamic changes in the space below in a visual way in keeping with the subject matter of the music (ice, wind, cold, seals). What composition you may have previously heard on this recording uses the same dynamic plan?

"Call of the Elephant" and "Under the Sun" have the same dynamic plan.

Name _____ Date _____

Student Page #11: *Ice Music (Part A)*

Directions:

1. Here are some names used to describe various types of ice in Antarctica: Green growler, new frazil fibrous, pancake, drift, and brash. Think about, and hypothesize (predict), what the different names mean, and how these names might have come about. Write your ideas on the chart below. Then, your teacher can tell you how close you came to being accurate.

See Antarctica in the CD booklet for background information on ice.

TYPE OF ICE	WHAT THE DIFFERENT NAMES MIGHT MEAN	HOW THESE NAMES MIGHT HAVE COME ABOUT	SOUNDS THAT EACH TYPE OF ICE MIGHT MAKE
green growler			
new frazil fibrous			
pancake			
drift			
brash			

Name _____ Date _____

Directions:

2. Bring some ice into the classroom and listen to the sounds it makes as you break it up into pieces. Then, again imagine the sounds that each type of ice might make and try to re-create these imagined sounds with available percussion instruments (cabasa, maracas, guiro, and so on) or other sound sources to create "ice music."

TYPE OF ICE	IDEAS FOR RECREATING THIS SOUND
green growler	
new frazil fibrous	
pancake	
drift	
brash	

3. Create your own "ice music." Begin and end with wind sounds. Use the *crescendo/decrescendo* effect you heard in *Antarctica.* Use two of your "ice music" sounds for Sound Sources #1 and #2. (See below.) Try to make "Sound Source #3 an animal sound associated with winter in your area (taped sounds of geese, winter birds, and so on). Develop your own chart, or use the format of *Antarctica* shown below. Tape your performance.

Sound Source #1 _____

Sound Source #2 _____

Sound Source #3 _____

0:00	Wind sound begins.
0:28	Sound Source #1 begins.
0:35	Sound Source #1 changes its sound in some way (or an additional sound source begins).
1:44	Sound Source #2 begins.
3:59	Sound Source #3 is heard.
4:03	Sound Source #3 stops.
4:58	Sound Source #2 stops.
5:05	Sound Source #1 (Only the wind is heard to the end.).
5:20	Wind stops.

Name _____ Date _____

Directions:
Find which organs in your town or area are pipe organs.

List two or three here.

‒‒

‒‒

‒‒

Find answers for the following questions. This will require individual or group research. If possible, go see one of these instruments and talk with the organist. Visit the loft where the pipes are housed. Listen to the instrument being played. Learn about the organ and how it is played. You may think of other things that you want to know about this instrument.

1. What are the names of some of the stops?
   Trumpet, Diapason, Strings, Oboe, Flute, Piccolo, Vox Humana (Human Voice). Some pipes are wood. Others are metal and have metal "tongues" that act like reeds of woodwind instruments. The number of pipes may range from several hundred to several thousand. There is a set of stops for each manual and one for the pedal board.

2. How do they work?
   The stop connects a particular set of pipes with the keys. Depressing a key forces air into an organ pipe. The air vibrates, causing the sound. They can be combined for different tone colors and can sound in octaves other than the one in which the organist is playing.

3. Why there are several keyboards (manuals)?
   For quick changes in tone color and for playing a melody on one manual, accompanied by softer sounds on another manual. The main manuals are called the "great," the "swell," and the "choir." Other manuals include "solo organ" and "echo organ."

4. How are the foot pedals played?
   With both feet. Organists often alternate between toe and heel as they move up and down. There is no sustaining pedal. The tone sounds only as long as a key is held down.

5. What are the reasons5
   for the different lengths of the pipes?
   The 8' pipes sound the same pitch as the piano. The 16' pipes sound an octave lower. The 32' pipes sound two octaves lower. The 4' pipes sound one octave higher. The 2' pipes sound two octaves higher.

6. How do the varying tone colors of the different ranks of pipes sound? (strings, diapason, reeds, trumpets, and so on)
   Answers may vary according to the student's opinion and ability to describe.

7. How are crescendi and decrescendi produced on a pipe organ?
   With the large pedals above the pedal board which open and close hidden shutters in front of the pipes.

8. When were pipe organs invented?
   The early Greeks invented early versions of organs, based on their pan pipes. The Romans used larger pipes, creating an instrument loud enough to be used in the coliseum as accompaniment for the gladiator fights. By A.D. 980, organs with bellows and keyboards were in use. Organs gradually developed enough to be used in the large cathedrals being built at that time. The highest point in the

5. OCEAN CHILD (THE OCEANS)
by Orca, Paul Halley, Paul Winter,
(Back Alley Music, ASCAP; Living Earth Music, BMI)

Outcome Choices:
1. Recording of improvised melodic questions and answers on Orff instruments, or other pitched instruments, using arpeggios in accompaniment. Taped for portfolio.
2. Improvised movement to suggest the movement of the whales, or use a shadow stick-puppet whale.
3. Written research on whales.
4. A script for an imaginary radio show based on their research (an interview of a renowned expert on whales).
5. Poems and/or songs about whales in the first person. These can be thought of as the lyrics of the song the whales "sing."

The First Hearing

Before:

Have the students
- Find the oceans on a map of the world.
- Listen as you read all or part of the information about this composition in the booklet included with the recording. Following are some highlights:
  Orca: Also known, somewhat incorrectly, as killer whales, average twenty feet in length and swim in every ocean. Their calls are audible through ten kilometers of open waters. They navigate with sonar clicks. The whales heard on the recording were taped in the Johnston Straits, British Columbia. They are probably a calf and its parents communicating with one another.
  Oceans: The upper ocean layers of phytoplankton produce half the world's oxygen. Each 300-400 million years the oceans completely cleanse themselves. Every 400-500 million years the Earth is made over.
  The Recording: Paul Winter actually recorded this "duet" live by hydrophone, from a canoe in the middle of the Johnston Straits.

During:

Have the students:
- Listen for the whale sounds.
- Decide what the sound of the piano accompaniment and soprano saxophone might represent. (Possible answers: the piano suggests the movement of the water; the soprano saxophone echoes the "songs" of the whales and portrays their gliding movements through the water.)

After:

Have the students:
- Discuss their ideas concerning what the piano and saxophone sounds might represent. (See above.)
- Identify the sound sources heard on the recording (orca, keyboards, soprano saxophone, cymbals).

Getting to Know the Music

Have the students:
- Listen carefully as you improvise simple spoken questions and answers with several class members (For example: "How are you doing today?" "I'm fine, thank you." "What did you have for lunch?" "I had a peanut butter sandwich.").

- Decide how the pitch at the end of a question is different from that at the end of an answer (A question usually ends with an upward inflection, while an answer usually ends with a downward inflection.)

- Listen as you, or a student, play upward and downward sounds on a slide whistle or other sound source, then try to echo them vocally.

- Listen to the music again, with attention to how the soprano saxophone echoes the upward and downward inflections of the various whale sounds.

Ecological Insights

<u>Blue whales</u> (Balaenoptera musculus) are thought to be the largest animals that have ever lived. They range from the tropics to the North Atlantic to the Arctic Ocean to around 85 degrees latitude, and south to Antarctica's Ross Sea.
<u>Humpback whales</u> (Megaptera novaeangliae) can be found in every ocean. They have well-defined migration patterns, from the cold northern waters of their feeding areas to their tropical and subtropical winter mating and calving grounds.
<u>Right whales</u> (Eubalaena glacialis) range from New England to the Davis Straits and Newfoundland, and in winter, from the coasts of Georgia and the Carolinas south to Florida and Bermuda.
<u>Gray whales</u> (Eschrichtius glaucus) summer in the northern and western Bering Sea where the waters are shallower. A few remain along the Pacific coast, while some venture to Alaska's Arctic Coast or off Siberia's northern coast. When the Arctic seas begin to freeze, the gray whales migrate south to the west coast of Baja California and into the California Gulf.

Background Information

The story of the orca-sax "duet"
Paul Winter describes recording this "duet" among a pod of orcas which was summering near Hansen Island in the Johnston Strait:

"We go in small boats into the Strait during the afternoon and wait for orcas. Far in the distance we see their blows, like puffs of musket-fire from a small brigade. As they come closer, diving and surfacing in regular cycles, we maneuver, so we'll be in their path. Through hydrophones [underwater microphones] trailing in the water we can hear their high-pitched cries. Our boat is a Baidarka - a three man kayak, with a sail and a dragonhead prow. I'm in the front port, playing the sax down into the water through an aluminum tube lashed to the kayak; Mickey Houlihan, our sound engineer, sits in the center with the recording gear on his lap; and Peter Johnson, with paddle, is in the rear.

When the orcas are within a few hundred yards I begin to imitate their calls. This I find fairly easy since many of their sounds are within the top range of the sax. We guess that the orcas can hear me since their hearing is so phenomenal, although I have no assurance of this. There are only a few times when it seems like their phrases are imitating or answering mine, but it's of little concern to me. I am thrilled just to *be* there, and to get to play along within the chorus of these magnificent beings."

Adolphe Sax (b. 1814) was a wind instrument player and maker whose father was a leading wind instrument maker in Brussels. He moved to Paris to establish his own workshop in 1842, and designed many improvements to different instruments. In 1846 he invented the **saxophone** which quickly became very popular, especially in military bands. The members of the saxophone family are: sopranino in Eb, soprano in Bb, alto in Eb, tenor in Bb, baritone in Eb, bass in Bb, and contrabass in Eb. Band master John Phillip Sousa introduced the saxophone to the U.S. in the 1890s.

- Dramatize the length of the orca by measuring twenty feet on the ground and marking it in some way. (Use the school hallway, if space does not permit this in the classroom.)

- Have some students do further research to find out more about the migratory paths of whales along the Atlantic and Pacific shores of the United States. Have them report their findings to the class.

- Have some students do research to find out about the dangers to the survival of whales that are caused by man, what is being done to remedy the problems, and what needs to be done in the future to protect them further.

- Have the students practice writing, reading, and orally improvising questions and answers on this subject, using complete sentences.

- Using their research as a basis, have the students work in groups to write scripts and enact an imaginary interview show, in which one student, playing the part of the interviewer (or several, working as a panel) asks questions on the subject of whales and other students, as the guest experts answer his/her questions.

- Create the visual suggestion of a whale moving through water by creating a stick-puppet figure of a whale and moving it behind a shadow screen. See notes for *Call of the Elephant* for rear-screen over head projector suggestions. (page #27) Water in the ocean can be suggested by laying a piece of blue transparency material on the overhead projector stage.

- Write poems about whales, using the first person. The poems can be thought of as the lyrics of the song the whales "sing." Some students may wish to set their poems to music and sing them.

Musical Discoveries

Distinguish Between Chords and Arpeggios (Student page #13)

Have the students:
- Play the following pitches simultaneously on any available pitched instruments. (If they are using instruments in which it is impossible for one person to play all of the pitches, have more than one student play. For example, on a metallophone, three students could each play one or two of the pitches shown.)

- Play the above pitches again, but this time play one note at a time, moving from one to the other as quickly as possible, in this manner:

- Clarify that in the first instance they were playing what are referred to as chords, and in the second they were playing what is called an arpeggio *(ahr - peh - zhoh)*, which means, in a "harp-like" manner.
- Listen for *arpeggios* played by the piano as they listen to *Ocean Child* again.
- Try playing arpeggios on various instruments — for example, on various Orff instruments, resonator bells, guitar, keyboard, piano, dulcimer, and so on. List those they can they play by themselves and those on which they play when they team up with others. Write their answers on **Student page #13**
- Try playing the arpeggio shown on **Student page #13**. Then, take turns playing it as an accompaniment as classmates improvise melodic "questions" and "answers" on other pitched instruments. (The rhythm of their arpeggio can be very free. In other words, it need not be rhythmically exact. It can represent the flow of the ocean as the improvised melodies represent conversations between various creatures of the ocean.)

Learn about the Soprano Saxophone (Student page #14)
Have the students:
- Read about Paul Winter, the soprano saxophone, and the saxophone family (soprano, alto, tenor, baritone, bass).

- Invite local students and/or community musicians to demonstrate the instruments of the saxophone family.

Improvise Musical Questions and Answers
Have the students:
- Improvise melodic questions and answers on Orff instruments, or other pitched instruments. (Avoid possible complications in improvising with *fa* and *ti* by using only do re mi so la of a major scale; for example, C D E G A in the Key of C major.).

- In pairs, alternate playing improvised melodies. One person plays a melodic "question" which ends with several upward-moving sounds. Tthe other person "answers" with a melody that ends with several downward-moving pitches.

Add an Arpeggiated Accompaniment to the Musical Questions and Answers
Have the students:
- Create an arpeggio-like accompaniment for the students' improvised melodies by setting up one or more Orff instruments or by using one or more sets of resonator bells. One person on each instrument plays upward and downward arpeggios in light, sweeping motions with the mallets. (This is particularly effective on an alto or bass metallophone but can also be achieved on the black keys of a piano, with the sweeping motions played with one hand while the damper pedal is held down to sustain the sounds. In this case, black keys must also be used for the melodic improvisation, in order to avoid dissonance [an incongruous sound] between the melody and the accompaniment. Black keys on melody bells, the piano, or any chromatic pitched instrument can be used to play the melody.)

FINAL EXPERIENCE: Have some class members improvise movement to suggest the swimming of the whales, or use a shadow stick-puppet whale, as suggested on the preceding page, or to their improvised question-and-answer melodies played over an arpeggiated accompaniment.

Name _____ Date _____

Student Page #13: *Transformations! Chords into Arpeggios!*

Directions:

1. Play the following pitches simultaneously on any available pitched instruments. (If you are using instruments in which it is impossible for one person to play all of the pitches, have more than one student play. For example, on a metallophone, three students could each play one or two of the pitches shown.)

2. Play the above pitches again, but this time play one note at a time, moving from one to the other as quickly as possible, in this manner:

In the first instance you were playing what are referred to as chords, and in the second you were playing what is called an *arpeggio (ahr - peh' - zhoh)*, which means, in a "harp-like" manner.

3. Listen for *arpeggios* played by the piano as you listen to *Ocean Child*.

4. Try playing *arpeggios* on various instruments — for example, on various Orff instruments, resonator bells, guitar, keyboard, piano, dulcimer, and so on.   Which can you play by yourself? Which can you play when you team up with others? Write your answers below.

5. Try playing this *arpeggio*. Take turns playing it as an accompaniment as classmates improvise melodic "questions" and "answers" on other pitched instruments. The rhythm of your *arpeggio* can be very free. In other words, it need not be rhythmically exact. Think of it as representing the flow of the ocean as the improvised melodies represent conversations between various creatures of the ocean. (Which creatures? Your group can decide!)

Student Page #14: *Paul Winter, the Soprano Saxophone and the Saxophone Family*

Adolphe Sax (b. 1814) was a wind instrument player and maker whose father was a leading wind instrument maker in Brussels. He moved to Paris to establish his own workshop in 1842, and designed many improvements to different instruments. In 1846 he invented the **saxophone** which quickly became very popular, especially in military bands. The members of the saxophone family are: sopranino in Eb, soprano in Bb, alto in Eb, tenor in Bb, baritone in Eb, bass in Bb, and contrabass in Eb. Band master John Phillip Sousa introduced the saxophone to the U.S. in the 1890s.

PAUL WINTER

Pioneer of a musical-ecological vision for the past 30 years, Paul Winter has followed a steady course toward his "Earth Music," a celebration of the creatures and cultures of the earth. Also known as "ecological jazz" and "living music," Winter's compositions are uniquely American in the widest sense, being rooted in European and African traditions and interweaving jazz, classical and folk elements with themes from the symphony of nature.

Artist-in-residence at New York's Cathedral of St. John the Divine, Paul Winter has also recorded in the evocative acoustic spaces of wilderness areas such as the Grand Canyon and Siberia's sacred Lake Baikal. "I think that the greatest contribution I could make as a musician would be to encourage people to make their own music," says Winter.

Paul Winter has released 27 recordings and received five Grammy nominations. He won a Grammy award in 1993 for his album, *Spanish Angel*. Honors in recognition for his work for the environment include awards from the World Wildlife Fund, the Humane Society and the United Nations Environment Program.

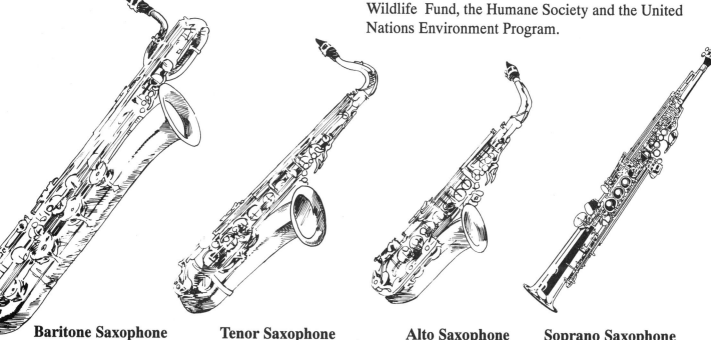

Baritone Saxophone   **Tenor Saxophone**   **Alto Saxophone**   **Soprano Saxophone**

6. UIRAPURÚ
DO AMAZONAS (South America)
by Gaudencio Thiago de Mello (Gau Publishing Co., BMI)

Outcome Choices:
1. Hand-made rain sticks.
2. Students play their own taped or improvised bird sounds with an instrumental accompaniment of their choice and making. The accompaniment could include their own hand-made rain sticks. (Tape the result for portfolios.)

The First Hearing

Before:
Have the students:
- Find out what species of birds inhabit the area in which they live and learn about the songs of some of these birds. (Answers will vary according to location.)
- Locate the Amazon River of Brazil on a map. (**Student page #15**)
- Listen as you tell them that in this composition they will hear a singer, Gaudencio Thiago de Mello, who has roots in the *Maue´* Indian tribe of the Amazon. The chant that he sings includes Nhinga Tu Indian dialect, Portuguese, and sounds imitating sounds of nature.
- Listen as you tell them that the bird they will hear, the *uirapurú*, is a tiny one, but has an amazingly intricate call and that there is a *Maue´* legend that anyone who hears the voice of this bird will live forever. The bird lives only in the rain forest.

During:
Have the students listen to the music, focusing on the sound of the *uirapurú* bird.

After:
Have the students compare the sound of the *uirapurú* bird to the sounds of the birds that inhabit their local area. (The sound of the *uirapurú* is probably much more complex and of a very clear tone color, closely resembling panpipes.)

Getting to Know the Music

Have the students:
- Listen and try to identify the instruments (guitar, rain stick, shaker, drum, whistles, soprano saxophone).
- Listen to notice that the bird almost does its own question/answer phrases. (It does not really do so, but the students can identify the same and different calls which may somewhat resemble their concept of question/answer phrases.)

Classroom Extensions

Have the students:
- Listen as you read to them about the Amazon rain forest in the booklet included with the recording. Explore with the students that the rain forest is not just one type of habitat, but includes many complex levels within different rain forest types, which makes the problem of saving rain forests all the more difficult.
- Find out more about the environmental issue of preserving the Amazon rain forests and report their findings to the class.
- Tape local bird sounds or find examples on records and tape them.

- Form pairs. Each pair is to create and write a question that the bird might ask related to its rain forest environment and an appropriate answer for the question. The answer may or may not come from the bird itself.

For example:

    Question: "What is happening to my wonderful rain forest?"
    Answer: "I can't begin to describe it."

Take turns reading their questions and answers.

Musical Discoveries

Make Their Own Rain Sticks

Have the students make their own rain sticks. Thoroughly seal up one end of a long cardboard tube (such as those on which paper gift wrapping is sold). Push dowel rods, pencils, or tongue depressors through the sides of the tube at about two-inch intervals. You will need to place them about an inch or two apart. Put tape around each stick to seal up each of the openings completely. Pour about one cup of popcorn, fine rice, grain, or pebbles into the tube and seal up the open end. Cover the tube with paper which the students have decorated in a colorful manner. Create the rain sound by slowly tilting the rain stick, causing the filler inside to gently tap against the rods inside the tube as the filler falls to the lower end. Continue by tilting the higher end downward once again. The effect simulates the restful sound of falling rain.

Learn to Play the Accompaniment Figure

Have the students:

- Step the rhythm of the ostinato accompaniment (♩ ♩ ♩) as they listen to the composition again.

- Take turns playing the pattern on bass xylophone, or other pitched instrument on these pitches:

(Note: The pitches in the guitar accompaniment on the recording [B C# F#] are not all on most classroom instruments (For example, a diatonic Orff instrument does not have a C#.). Therefore, the pattern shown is intended only for accompanying the melodic improvisation explained below. It cannot be played with the recording.)

Other Latin American instruments can be added to this accompaniment pattern. Have the players create their own patterns, or use some, or all, of the following:

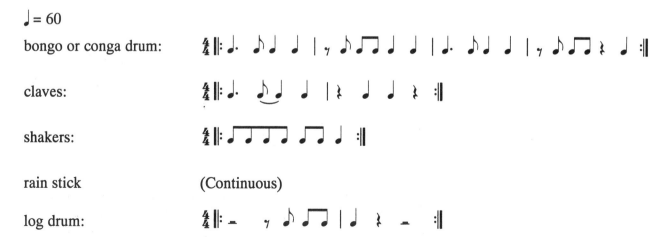

Improvise Melodies

Have the students:

• Set up Orff instruments, or other pitched instruments with G Bb C D F G.

• Take turns playing their own short tunes; then, immediately sing what they have just played, using a neutral syllable.

• Take turns playing question and answer phrases on pitched instruments (such as alto xylophone and glockenspiel) while one student plays the accompaniment pattern (see above) on bass xylophone or other pitched instrument.

(Ask the students to make their improvised phrases the length of four repetitions of the accompaniment pattern [sixteen beats] and to end questions on D and answers on G.)

• One or more dancers might wish to express the spirit of the *uirapurú* bird through free improvised movement.

• Use the written questions and answers created above as an introduction to the improvisation, spoken by each person over a soft tremolo G (rapid, repeated notes played with alternating hands.)

FINAL EXPERIENCE: Have the students play their own taped or improvised bird sounds with an instrumental accompaniment of their choice. The accompaniment could include their own hand-made rain sticks.

Name _____ Date _____

Student Page #15: *Map of South America*

Directions: Fill in each rectangle, correctly labelling the geographic feature to which each is related. Work alone, or in small groups, as directed by the teacher.

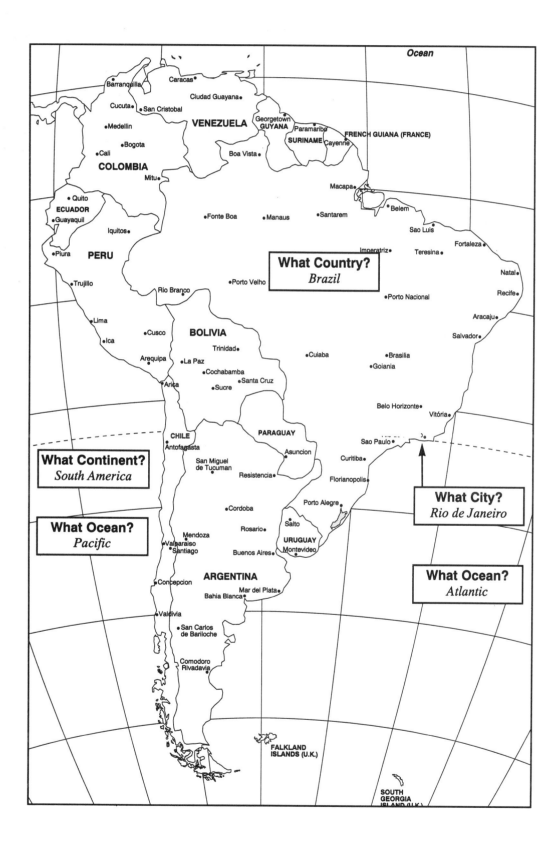

7. Talkabout (Australia)

by Steve Turre, Paul Winter, Eugene Friesen, Russ Landau
(Living Earth Music, BMI)

Outcome Choices:
1. Hand-made instruments in the style of Aborigines.
2. Essays or poems on the plight of the Aborigines.
3. Recording of play-along, preceded by the reading of one or more of their essays or poems.

The First Hearing

Before:

Have the students label Australia on the map. (**Student page #16**) Then, give them the following information about the lyrebird and the didjeridu, both of which are heard in this composition:

The lyrebird is so named because the tail of the male bird resembles a spectacular musical lyre. The tail appears at first to be a rather drab brown; but when it is raised above its head it reveals a shimmering underside of silver. The lyrebird is able to imitate other birds, supplementing its own beautiful melodic calls. (Ask the students to listen for a "bob-white" at the end of this selection!)

Lyrebird

During:

Have the students listen for, and identify, the lyrebird and the didjeridu as well as other sounds heard on the recording (sticks, soprano saxophone, bull-roarers).

After:

• Discuss sound sources they identified.

Getting to Know the Music

Have the students make Aborigine-style instruments: (**Student page #17**)

Didjeridu - A long cardboard tube, such as that used to hold gift-wrap, can be used for a simple didjeridu. First, teach the students to "buzz" with their lips, by lightly pressing them together and blowing through them, creating a sound. Then they can do the same with the tube to their mouths. This is how sound is produced on brass instruments (trumpet, trombone, French horn, tuba, etc.).

Sticks - Any resonant, hard wood (for example, dowel rods) can be used to fashion sticks similar to those heard on the recording.

Bull-roarer - This is one of the most ancient instruments known, dating back more than 25,000 years. It is found throughout the world. Some cultures believe that bull-roarers are the voices of their ancestors. To make one, form an elongated oval shape from wood about six to ten inches long. Make a hole in one end and tie a sturdy string through it. Make sure you have plenty of room, hold the free end of the string and swing the bull-roarer around overhead, creating a whining sound. See if the pitch changes when whirling it faster or slower.

Classroom Extensions

• Have the students do research to find out more about Aborigines and how their culture has been threatened by the encroachment of outsiders. Have them share their findings with the class through essays and/or poems.

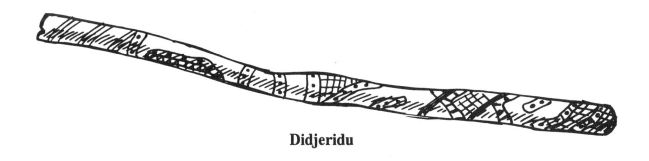

Didjeridu

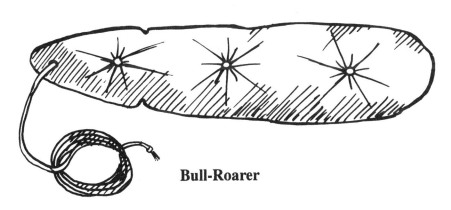

Bull-Roarer

Australian Aborigines

The word aborigine is from the Latin, meaning from the very first. Aboriginal people are the earliest known inhabitants of a country or region. About 20,000 years BCE, Borneo, Sumatra, Java and Bali - now islands - were joined as part of an area of Old Melanesia called Sundaland. Even before the end of the last Ice Age, the ancestors of the Aborigines were crossing the Timor Strait from Sundaland into what is now New Guinea and Australia.

The Aborigines believe that all life forms are part of an inter-connecting web of relationships stemming from the Dreamtime. The Dreamtime is the mythological era of creation, out-of-time, when the Spirit Ancestors molded the Australian landscape. The power of the dreamtime is still present as the journeys of the ancestors are re-enacted in ceremonies and dance.

Didjeridu

Music and dance are essential to the daily life of the Australian Aborigines. The didjeridu (did-jeh-ree-doo') is a type of very ancient wind instrument that is still played by the Aborigines of northern Australia. It is made in an ingenious way: A eucalyptus or gum-tree branch about six feet long is buried in the ground so that termites will bore out its core. The resulting hollow tube is dug out and decorated.

It is blown like a trumpet with loosely vibrating lips, and, using mouth and tongue, can produce an amazingly varied range of tone colors and rhythmic patterns. A drone can be sustained using a technique called circular breathing. The didjeridu can imitate sounds from nature, and gives the cue for movements in highly stylized ritual dances. Apart from the bullroarer, other percussive instruments used by the Australian Aborigines are sticks and boomerangs clacked together.

In this recording, the didjeridu is played by Steve Turre, a trombonist on the television show, "Saturday Night Live."

Lyrebird (Family Mervridae)

Lyrebirds live in the mountain forests of southeastern Australia, from southeast Queensland to Victoria. They spend most of their lives on the ground, but will flap into a tree to roost. They feed on insects and larvae which they rake up with their strong legs and feet. The lyrebird has a repertoire of beautiful bubbling melodies, supplemented with perfect imitations of other voices. The male builds a large camouflaged mound of grass. He leaps on top to display his lyre-shaped tail to a female, flipping the tail over his head and revealing its shimmering underside.

Play-Along With Instruments They Have Made

Have the students play along with the recording on their own instruments. (Total time of the composition: 3:52.)

Didjeridu: Rhythms similar to the following (0:16 to 3:00 of elapsed time). Long, sustained sounds from (3:00 to 3:30).

Sticks: The following (1:55 to 3:00 of elapsed time):

Bull Roarer: The following (2:11 to 3:00 of elapsed time):

FINAL EXPERIENCE: Have the students accompany the recording on their instruments. Precede the performance with a the reading of one of their essays or poems on the plight of the Aborigines.

Name _____ Date _____

Student Page #16: *Map of Australia*

Directions: Fill in each rectangle, correctly labelling the geographic feature to which each is related. Work alone, or in small groups, as directed by the teacher.

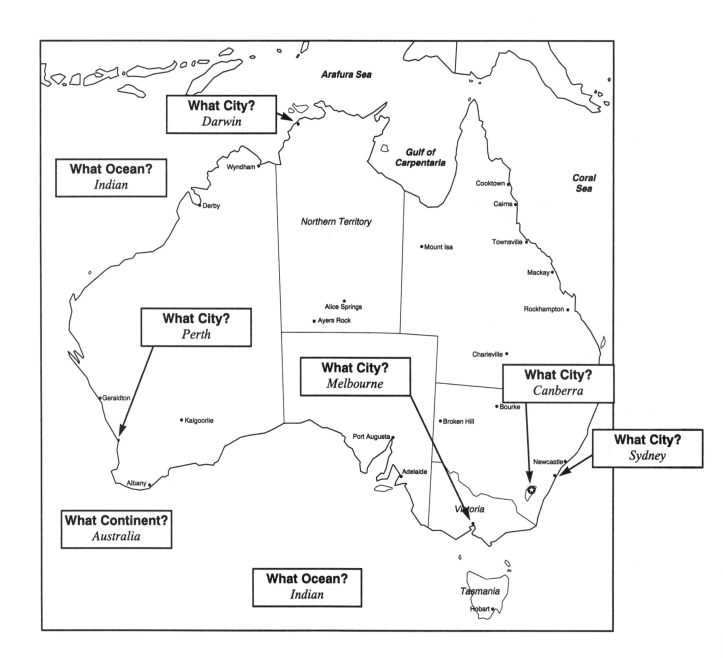

Name _____ Date _____

Student Page #17: *Making Instruments in the Aborigine Style*

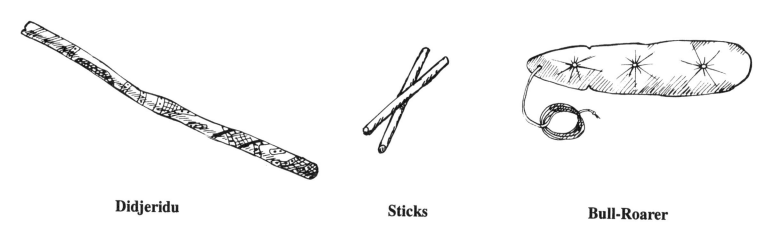

Didjeridu   **Sticks**   **Bull-Roarer**

Directions:

Didjeridu - A long cardboard tube, such as that used to hold gift-wrap, can be used for a simple didjeridu. First, learn to "buzz" with your lips, by lightly pressing them together and blowing through them, creating a sound. Then do the same with the tube to your mouth. This is how sound is produced on brass instruments. Among the Aborigines, only men are permitted to play the didjeridu.

Sticks - Any resonant, hard wood (for example, dowel rods) can be used to fashion sticks similar to those heard on the recording.

Bull-Roarer - This is one of the most ancient instruments known, dating back more than 25,000 years. It is found throughout the world. Some cultures believe that bull-roarers are the voices of their ancestors. To make one, form an elongated oval shape from light wood or heavy cardboard, about six to ten inches long. Make a hole in one end and tie a sturdy string through it. Making very sure that you have plenty of room, hold the free end of the string and swing the bull-roarer around overhead, creating a whining sound. Change the pitch by whirling it faster or slower.

Play-Alongs
Directions: Play these rhythms on the instruments you have made as you listen to *Talkabout*.

Didjeridu: Rhythms similar to the following (0:16 to 3:00 of elapsed time).
Long, sustained sounds from (3:00 to 3:30).

Sticks: The following (1:55 to 3:00 of elapsed time):

Bul-Roarer: The following (2:11 to 3:00 of elapsed time):

8. RUSSIAN GIRLS (A WEDDING SONG) (ASIA)
by Dimitri Pokrovsky, Paul Winter, Eugene Friesen, Russ Landau, and Paul Halley
(Living Earth Music, BMI)

The First Hearing

Outcome Choices:
1. Students create their own patterns in 5/4.
2. Recording of students' play-along patterns with Russian Girls.
3. Research on threatened wilderness areas.

Before:

Have the students:

• Find Russia, and the other areas named in the CD booklet, on the map. **(Student page #18)**

• Listen as you tell them the following about the Dimitri Pokrovsky Singers.
(This group of young folk singers, based in Moscow, is dedicated to preserving the living traditions of Russian village music. They are featured with the Paul Winter Consort on the album, *EARTHBEAT*. The two ensembles have toured together, both in the U.S.A. and in Russia.)

• About the song: In this wedding song from Pskov, in the north of Russia, the women sing from a centuries-old village tradition. A song sung to a bride at a wedding by her family and friends is a frequently encountered type of folk song in Russia, as well as in a number of other Eastern European countries.

• About this performance: The song will be heard in a new and non-traditional way through the addition of a new melody and accompaniment woven around it by the Paul Winter Consort. Because of the narrow range of the vocal melody and the repetition of its melodic and rhythmic patterns, Paul Winter felt that this type of folk song would lend itself to being complemented by the contemporary sounds of the Consort. The result is a unique combination of folk and composed material blended into a completely new style.

During:

Have the students:

• Follow the translation as they listen to the music with its Russian text. Photocopy page 63 for students so that they may follow the translation as they listen to the music with its Russian text.
(Translation by Leonid B. Pereversev).

• Listen for the two styles of music: traditional folk and newly-composed.

• Listen to identify any instruments they can, and to determine if the singers are heard throughout. (They are not.)

The Dimitri Pokrovsky Singers

After:
- Discuss the composition with regard to:
  — the effect of the combination of styles.
  — the instruments they recognize. (soprano saxophone, cello, keyboards, drum and shakers, bass. The cellist, Eugene Friesen, sings what he plays, but the two timbres are so blended that this may be difficult for them to discern.)
  — whether the singers were heard throughout. (No. There is a middle section with instruments only.)
  — what the combination of styles conveys about living in Asia and the world at this time. (Accept all thoughtful answers. There is increasing interaction and communication between cultures that have been formerly widely separated and unknown to one another. The ultimate result will be a blending of cultures not before possible.)
- Discuss what the combination of styles might seem to convey about living in Asia and in the world in this period of time.

Getting to Know the Music

Have the students:
- Listen to the music again to hear instruments and other details they may have missed. (For example: the almost hymn-like quality of the section with instruments alone [2:12 to 2:38 of elapsed time]; the contrast between this part and the more rhythmic music that accompanies the singers; the resultant over-all ABA form.

Classroom Extensions

Have the students:
- Listen as you read all or part of the information on the former U.S.S.R. in the booklet accompanying the recording.
- Discuss the problems caused by countries that disrupt the fragile balance of wilderness areas. Do research on this issue. Share their research.

Discover and Practice in 5/4 Meter

Have the students:

- Listen to discover the 5/4 meter (Pat on the down beats. Then counting the down beat as beat one, count the intervening beats.)
- Listen again, patting a simple 5/4, all-quarter note pattern. (Use **optional student page**)
- Form small groups. Each group is to decide on a body percussion combination for a pattern in 5/4 with one sound for each beat, notate it, and practice it with the recording.

    NOTE: Experienced classes may use several slightly more complex rhythms in 5/4 meter and choose two instruments on which to play them. Two examples:

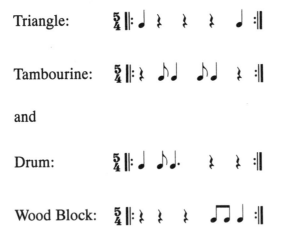

Triangle:

Tambourine:

and

Drum:

Wood Block:

FINAL EXPERIENCE: Choose a conductor to indicate during the music when each group is to play its pattern with the recording. Precede it by having some students share their research on the fragility of wilderness areas.

A Russian Wedding Song in 5/4

This is a wedding song from Pskov, in the north of Russia.
(Translation by Leonid B. Pereversev.).

	English	**Russian**
CHORUS:	You, our wise one ---	Наша умная раэумная,
	You, our clever one ---	Наша гихая-смирёюıая,
	You, our modest one.	Наша девица, паша Аннушка,
		Наша девица Алексеевна.
1.	What makes you look so sad?	Она иила уэор, эолотом,
	(Chorus repeated.)	Вышивала мистым серебром.
2.	Do tell us what's on your mind.	Недошила уэор, бросила,
	(Chorus repeated.)	А сама горко эаплакала.
3.	Oh, now we come to understand . . .	Уж ты батюшка. роцитсĿ мой
	(Chorus repeated.)	Эацрайй ты свой широкнй двор
4.	Oh, now you're about to leave us,	Вижу, едет непрцятеĿ мой.
	your family and loving friends.	НепрнятеĿ, цобрый молоцсц,
	(Chorus repeated.)	Добрнй молодец иванушка,
5.	Oh, now you're about to start a long,	Добрнй молодец Сергеевнч.
	long way of your own.	
	(Chorus repeated.)	

An Improvisation in 5/4

1. Form small groups. Each is to create a five-beat body percussion pattern. It is to be all quarter notes. (For example: Pat Clap Snap L. Snap R. Clap) Write your body percussion pattern in the space below. Then, do the pattern with your group as you listen for the 5/4 meter in *Russian Girls*.

$\frac{5}{4}$ ‖: _____ _____ _____ _____ _____

2. Listen again, having only one group at a time perform their pattern. A conductor can indicate when each group is to perform.

3. Try playing these slightly more complex rhythms in 5/4 meter on two instruments.

Triangle: $\frac{5}{4}$ ‖: ♩ 𝄽 𝄽 𝄽 ♩ :‖

Tambourine: $\frac{5}{4}$ ‖: 𝄽 ♫ ♫ ♩ 𝄽 :‖

Drum: $\frac{5}{4}$ ‖: ♩ ♪♩. 𝄽 𝄽 :‖

Wood Block: $\frac{5}{4}$ ‖: 𝄽 𝄽 𝄽 ♫ ♩ :‖

4. Choose two different instruments to play your group's pattern. Write the instruments you have chosen to play and notation for what they will play, below. Try playing your pattern with the recording.

Instrument #1:_____ $\frac{5}{4}$ ‖:   :‖

Instrument #2:_____ $\frac{5}{4}$ ‖:   :‖

(Permission to photocopy)

Name _____ Date _____

Student Page #18: *Map of Russia*

Directions: Fill in each rectangle, correctly labelling the geographic feature to which each is related. Work alone, or in small groups, as directed by the teacher. Find out what you can about the fragility of the wilderness areas in this part of the world. Share your findings with the class.

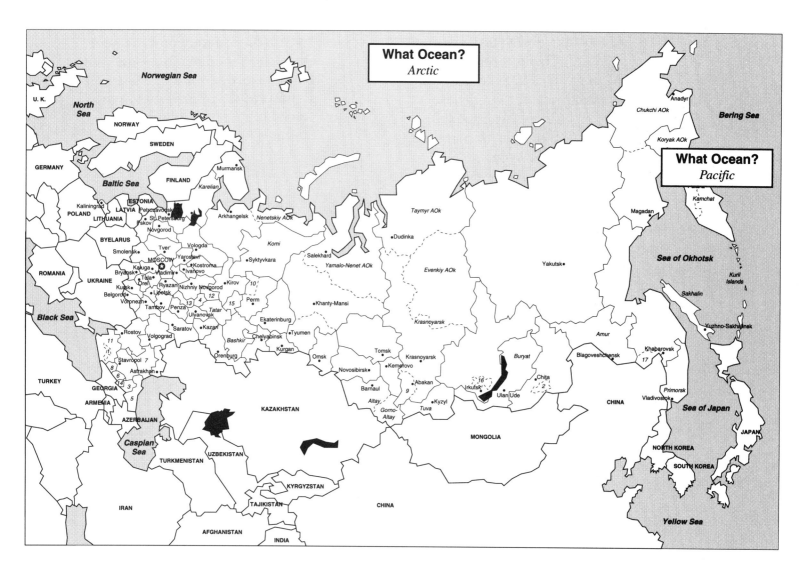

9. *BLACK FOREST (EUROPE)*
by Paul Winter (Living Earth Music, BMI)

Outcome Choices: 1. Students research the history of, and literature set in, the Black Forest.
2. Stories about an imaginary present-day person who saves the Black Forest from destruction.
3. Trios created in the style of the music by improvising on melody instruments to the accompaniment of taped bird and water sounds that you have gathered. (This could be enhanced by projecting slides of the birds whose sounds they have taped. It could also be used as background for one of their stories, detailed above.)
4. Recordings of their improvisations and stories.

The First Hearing

Before:
Have the students:
• Tell what they know about the Black Forest (The *Schwarzwald,* along the east bank of the Rhine river, in Germany.) and the fairy tales and other magical legends associated with it (for example, the Grimm Brothers tales such as *Hansel and Gretel*).
• Find Germany, and the area in which the forest is located, on the map. **(Student page #19)**
• Listen as you tell them that the music they will hear is a trio, remembering what a trio must contain (three sound sources.).

During:
• Listen to the music, imagining they are walking through the Black Forest.
• Listen for and identify the three sound sources that make it a trio.

After:
• Name the sound sources used that make it a trio: (Bird + Water + Soprano Saxophone = A trio!)

Getting to Know the Music

Have the students:
Discuss other things they noticed about the music, listening again, as necessary, to verify their discoveries.
(For example: There is no other accompaniment, and no real meter. The rhythm is in an improvisational style. The bird is heard throughout the composition. The melody heard at the beginning is repeated near the end.)

Classroom Extensions

Have the students:
• Listen as you read all or part of the information in the booklet included with the recording on the Black Forest and about how the forest is dying.
• Discuss this problem and what can be done by individuals and governments to help alleviate it.
• Depending on the age of the class and their level of interest, read — or at least mention — one or more stories that are associated with the Black Forest (for example, such Grimm Brothers' stories as *The Bremen Town Musicians, Little Red Riding Hood, Rumplestiltskin, Sleeping Beauty, Snow White and the Seven Dwarves*). Older students might enjoy selecting one of the stories to read to first or second graders.
• Make tapes of natural water and bird sounds in their area and bring them in to share with the class.

- In groups of four, write their own stories about an imaginary present-day person who saves the Black Forest from destruction.
- Tape bird and natural water sounds in their own environment. If possible, put each on separate tapes and arrange for two cassette tape players for a later performance. (Bird calls, or pre-recorded tapes — available in stores specializing in natural items — may be substituted for their gathering their own bird calls and water sounds.)

Ecological Insights

The European Blackbird (Turdus merula) is a member of the thrush family of songbirds, and one of the commonest birds of the region. The male is a distinctive jet-black with bright orange-yellow bill. It has a mellow fluty call. The female is dark brown with lighter underparts. She incubates her eggs in a nest of plant material lined with mud. The blackbird lives in both broad-leaved and coniferous forests, in woods, parks, gardens, and orchards, and feeds on invertebrates, berries and plant matter.

Musical Discoveries

Improvise a Trio on Melody Instruments. (see **Student page #20:** *A Black Forest Rescue*)
Have the students:
- Learn to play the following on recorder or other pitched instrument (Some students who are studying other instruments should be strongly encouraged to use their instruments, if the instrument would be appropriate for the subject and mood. The theme is an adaptation of the opening of Paul Winter's solo in Black Forest, page 67. (Permission to photocopy)

- Create a trio in a similar style to the music. Take turns improvising in D la pentatonic on recorder or other pitched instrument. (D F G A C D') to the accompaniment of their taped bird and natural water sounds they have found in their own environment. If possible, have the bird and water sounds on two different tapes and two different recorders so they can be brought in or out at will by the performers by adjusting the volume. Use the above theme, played by one or more persons, as a recurring main theme between each improvisation. Try to maintain the same mood and serious intent of the theme in all of the improvisations.

FINAL EXPERIENCE: Have the students improvise on melody instruments, as suggested above, to the accompaniment of taped bird and water sounds that they have gathered. This could be enhanced by projecting slides of the birds whose sounds they have taped. The improvisations could be used as background for the story they have created. In groups of four, one could be the reader as the others perform (the pitched instrument improviser and two persons manipulating the tape players.).

A Bird of the Black Forest

<u>The European Blackbird</u> (Turdus merula) is a member of the thrush family of songbirds, and one of the commonest birds of the region. The male is a distinctive jet-black with bright orange-yellow bill. It has a mellow fluty call. The female is dark brown with lighter underparts. She incubates her eggs in a nest of plant material lined with mud. The blackbird lives in both broad-leaved and coniferous forests, in woods, parks, gardens, and orchards, and feeds on invertebrates, berries and plant matter.

BLACK FOREST

PAUL WINTER

(Permission to photocopy)

rit.

Name _____ Date _____

Student Page #19: *Map of Germany*

Directions: Fill in each rectangle, correctly labelling the geographic feature to which each is related. Work alone, or in small groups, as directed by the teacher.

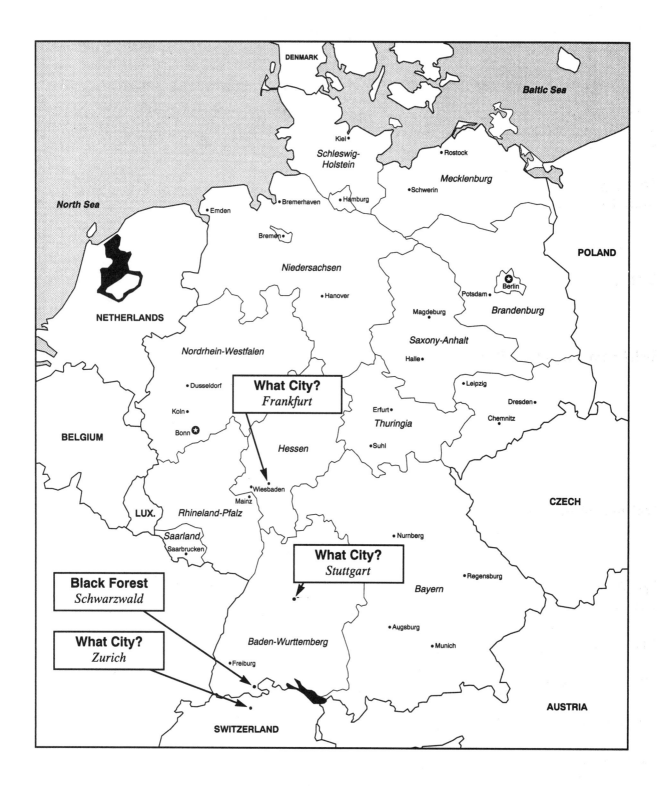

Name _____ Date _____

Student Page #20: *A Black Forest Rescue (Story and Improvised Trio Accompaniment)*

Directions:
In groups of four, write a story about an imaginary present-day person who saves the Black Forest from destruction. Then, plan a trio to accompany the reading of your story. The trio will consist of one person improvising on a pitched instrument, one person responsible for bird sounds, and a third person responsible for water sound effects. You may need two tape recorders, with the bird sounds on one and the water sounds on the other, so the sounds of the bird and the water can be brought in or out at will by the performers by adjusting the volume.

Use this page to summarize your plans. When your teacher has seen and approved these preliminary plans, gather the sound effects and practice the improvisation. Try to maintain the same mood and serious intent of the theme in all of the improvisations. Rehearse the reading of the story with the improvisation. When you are ready, perform the story with the improvisation and sound effects for the class.

Story Outline
Main Characters:

Setting:

Brief Summary of the Plot:

Outcome of the Story:

Trio Plans
Pitched Instrument to be Used:_____

Name of Player:_____

Plans for bird sounds:_____

Person responsible:_____

Plans for water sounds:_____

Person responsible:_____

10. SONG OF THE EXILE
by Gaudencio Thiago de Mello (Gau Publishing Co., BMI)

The First Hearing

Outcome Choices: 1. Interviews of local people who were once in political exile.
2. Essays of students own experiences of being exiled.
3. Shakers that students make out of natural substances or re-cycled materials.

Before:

Have the students:

• Look up the word "exile" and discuss its meaning.
• Listen as you tell them that they will hear a song by Thiago de Mello, who was forced into self-exile from Brazil in 1966 by a military dictatorship. (He also performs on another selection on this recording, *Uirapurú Do Amazonas*, singing and playing guitar, rain stick, drum and whistles through multi-track recording techniques.)
• Locate Brazil on the map (see **Student page #15**).
• Listen as you read the English translation of the words. Ask them to watch for a non-English word.

SONG OF THE EXILE
Music and Lyrics by Gaudencio Thiago de Mello

English (literal translation)

I built myself a boat from hope,
out of pain, made sea.
From injustice I wrought a strong oar
to take me to a safe port.

I strung letters into a thousand words
to be a vehicle for my thinking.
Instead of weeping I wrote a verse,
but I must be free to sing it.

I fashioned dawn out of a fire,
from the ashes made the sun rise,
but it was what I felt for my beloved
that birthed this song inside.

It is the sun, the sea,
my *boi-bumba´*,
the rhythm of the dance in me.
My suffering will end
I'm sure I'll live in peace up there.

Portuguese

Fiz um barco da esperança
E das dores, fiz um mar.
Da injustiça, um remo forte
Para um porto me levar.

Fiz das letras mil palavras
Pra´ seguir o meu pensar
Fiz um verso, em vez de pranto
Mas ser livre pra cantar.

Fiz do fogo uma alvorada
E das cinzas, um clarão
Mas o amor pra minha amada
Fez em mim esta conção

E´ sol, e´ mar
E´ meu boi-bumba´.
E´ sol, e´ mar
E´ meu boi-bumba´.

- Identify the non-English word (*boi-bumba´*)
- Decide why it is not translated (Some words cannot be translated because their meanings cannot be duplicated exactly in other languages. *Boi-bumba´* is a dance rhythm.).

During:

Have the students listen to the song, thinking about its meaning and listening for *boi-bumba´*, when it occurs.

After:

- Have the students talk about how they would feel if they were exiled from their home country. Share experiences similar to being exiled that they may have had. Think of areas around the world in which people are currently leaving their homelands and moving to other countries. (Some may only be able to relate how they felt after being sent to their rooms. Others may be able to share experiences of actually having to leave their homes and/or countries. Encourage students to share their feelings, whatever the situation.)

Background Information

Thiago de Mello explains that *boi-bumbá* is a folk rhythm for a dance. It is also an event in the north of Brazil which involves a dance with a bull. The bull "dies" a ritual death, and then is miraculously revived by the medicine man. Thiago thinks of *boi-bumbá* in the song as being related to his anguish, and to his desire that — after the military dictatorship — there would be democracy. It is also his personal "phoenix" — his hope to come to a new land as if to be reborn to the possibilities of a new life.

Getting to Know the Music

Have the students:
- Listen again to try to identify the instruments on the recording.
- List the instruments they can identify, then supplement their lists with those from the list of instruments actually used: keyboards, soprano saxophone, guitar, cocoon shakers, *cis* (Amazon gourd), *surdo* (Brazilian drum), *agogo* bells (two-tone bells).
- Listen again for instruments they did not hear previously.

Classroom Extensions

Have the students:
- Write about their own experiences of being exiled; why it happened; how it made them feel.
- Reflect on and discuss possible reasons for including this song on a recording dealing with environmental issues (One possibility: As we become more conscious about protecting the environment, we will also become more sensitive to the right of all peoples to live in dignity and freedom. Military dictatorships make this impossible for many forced to live under them.)
- Interview a person in their community who has at one time been a political exile. (**Student page #21**)

Musical Discoveries

Make Instruments to Play With the Recording (Student page #22)
Have the students:
- Find natural shakers, such as cocoons or seed pods, or create them out of materials at hand.
- Practice playing a steady eighth-note rhythm

    at the tempo of the beginning of the recording ($\quarternote$ = 88-92).
- Play with the recording, noticing the tempo changes and adjusting their playing as necessary, in order to stay with the singer.

FINAL EXPERIENCE:
Have some of the students read their essays about exile and share their interviews.
Have them listen to the recording and play along on shakers.

THE EXILE SONG

Music and Lyrics by
THIAGO DeMELLO

Name _____ Date _____

Student Page #21: *Interview Outline*

Directions: For this project, you will begin by doing research to find a person in your community who has at one time been a political exile. Someone in your own family may be an exile. If not, you will need to ask friends and relatives to help you find this person. You might find help with a local newspaper, minister, or social services center. Put your preliminary plans on this form. When it has been approved by the teacher, conduct your interview. Tape it, if possible, and share the recording with the class. Be sure that you have the person's permission to tape what they say before doing so. Try to take a camera along to the interview so that you can have a picture of the person. Consider video-taping the interview.

Section 1: Preliminary Information

Name of Interviewee_____

Address of Interviewee_____

Telephone of Interviewee_____

Referred by (Name and Position)_____

Date of Planned Interview_____

Name of Adult Who Will Accompany You on the Interview_____

Section 2: Interview Plans

Do you plan to:

Take a camera for still pictures?   Yes_____   No_____

Take a video-camera for video-taping the interview?   Yes_____   No_____

Questions you plan to ask:

1.

2.

3.

4.

5.

Other Comments or Plans:

Name _____ Date _____

Directions: The instruments pictured are those native to Brazil that are heard on the recording of *Song of the Exile,* along with soprano saxophone, guitar and keyboards. Listen for these instruments when you hear *Song of the Exile.*

Surdo Drums

Agogo Bells

Re-Cycled Shakers

Find natural shakers, such as cocoons or seed pods, or create shakers out of materials at hand (Re-cycled insturments!). Use them to accompany *Song of the Exile*, playing a steady eighth-note rhythm at the beginning, then adjusting the tempo as necessary throughout the recording, in order to stay with the singer-composer, Guadencio Thiago de Mello.

11. UNDER THE SUN (Desert)
by Paul Winter, Glen Velez, John Clark, Paul McCandless, Paul Halley
(Living Earth Music, BMI)

Outcome Choices:
1. Pictures of different stages of sunset in the desert.
2. Descriptive writings of sunsets on the desert, with instrumental accompaniment sounds to enhance and dramatize the meaning of the words. (Tape the results.)
3. Performance of the students' spoken and musical descriptions as an introduction, then move to the recording and/or their own improvisations.

The First Hearing

Before:

Have the students
- Relate what they may already know about the desert.
- Find principal desert areas on the map. (**Student page #23**)
- Predict what music about sunset on the desert would sound like.

During:
- Have them silently test their predictions against what they hear.

After:

Have the students:
- Compare what they heard in the music with their predictions of how it would sound.
- Speculate on what they think the drum might represent. (A camel? A person walking through the sand?)
- Read the description of the composition. (**Student page #24**).

Getting to Know the Music

Have the students:
- Listen again and identify the instruments they hear (soprano saxophone, French horn, oboe, pipe organ, shaker, and bendir [a desert drum which has a characteristic buzzing sound]. (**Student page #24**)
- Identify the only instrument not playing sustained sounds. (The drum.)
- Become better acquainted with the composition by listening to identify the elapsed times when:

a. The drum is heard.   (From 0:20 to 2:00 and from 4:40 to 5:27, the end.)

b. The loudest point is reached.   (At about 4:10 to 4:25)

Classroom Extensions

Have the students:
- Draw pictures of different stages of a sunset in the desert. First, discuss what these stages might be, then have each student or group of students draw one stage of the sunset, ending with a night scene. (Suggestion: Use the description of a sunset on **Student page #24** for ideas.).
- Write their own descriptions of sunset on the desert, then add the instrumental sounds of their choice to enhance and dramatize the meaning of the words.
- Do research on the undesired "desertification" of areas of the world. Find the causes for this, where it is happening, what can be done to alleviate the problem, what the outcome will be when nothing is done.
- After reflecting on this issue, write their thoughts on it.

Deserts

Often deserts have a negative image as 'wastelands', but they are important, delicately balanced ecosystems, with many plants and creatures superbly adapted to live in them. Not all deserts are hot and sandy; the Gobi in central Asia and the Great Basin in North America are cold deserts that lie in the higher latitudes. Deserts grow where there is little and infrequent rain, and high evaporation. Some desert areas form because they are far from the sea and rain clouds shed their load before reaching them, or because mountains block them off from moisture laden winds. Intense human activity ill-suited to drier soils such as over-grazing, over-cultivation and salination of soils from irrigation, has contributed to desertification. Cycles of drought can also severely desiccate a vulnerable region, but usually are short-lived, although desert climates do change over time. For example, prehistoric cave drawings show that between 7,000 to 4,000 years ago, elephants, rhinoceroses, crocodiles and hippopotamuses used to live in the now barren Saharan highlands.

The ability to obtain and conserve water is paramount for survival in the desert. Plants tend to have small, wax coated or hairy leaves that can withstand heat and limit moisture loss. Some plants bloom at night, where there is an abundance of insects, or when nectar-eating bats will pollinate the flowers. Some plants develop a wide-spreading shallow root system to draw water from a large radius; others send a long tap-root to extract moisture from deep underground. Cacti and other succulent plants store water in their fleshy stems.

Animals have different strategies for life in the desert, such as sheltering by day in holes or under rocks, burrowing into cool, moist deep tunnels, and storing food in case of drought. Dormancy, torpidity, camouflage, and efficient kidneys are other special physical adaptations. Other examples for survival: desert rodents such as jerboas and gerbils obtain the water they need solely from their diet; the ostrich has nasal glands that excrete salt, enabling it to drink salty water; the fennec fox has very long ears that conduct heat away from the body; lizards can store food in their fat tails, and their thick skin shields them from dehydration; large mammals such as the Addax antelope can tolerate the day-time rise in temperature by storing excess body heat until the evening, when it is lost as the air cools.

The Camel (Family Camelidae) can store water in its body tissues and accumulate fat reserves in its hump, which also protects from sun by absorbing heat. The Bacterian camel (Camelus ferus) of the Gobi Desert has two humps. The Camel sheds its coat in summer, but grows long shaggy hair to protect it from the winter cold. The Dromedary (Camelus dromedarius) has one hump. It used to roam wild in North Africa and Arabia until it was domesticated, probably around 4,000 BC. The camel's feet are highly specialized for its desert environment, having two toes and two flat broad pads on each foot and a nail on top of each toe, enabling it to roam easily over the soft soils.

Camel

79

Become Aware of Additional Musical Features

Have the students:

- Discover the free meter in all instruments except the drum.
- Discover the long *crescendo - decrescendo* effect.
- Plot the *crescendo - decrescendo* effect on the board, then follow it as they listen.
- Move with the music to show the *crescendo - decrescendo*, expressing the feeling evoked by the desert sunset. Suggestion: Use long crepe paper streamers of different sunset colors. Begin with the streamers being gathered in a box in the center of a circle of dancers. Each dancer can take the end of one of the streamers, gradually move away from the center as the music becomes louder, then gradually move back to the center as they gather up their streamers and return them to the box — thus, simulating and demonstrating visually the effect of a *crescendo - decrescendo.*). This effect can be enhanced by gradually increasing, then reducing, the amount of light in the room (adjusting window shades, lights, and so on) with colored spots, or colored transparencies in sunset colors on an overhead projector that has been turned so that the dancers are bathed in its light.

Learn the Drum Pattern

(The drum pattern requires two different pitches played on a single drum. This is done by playing in the middle of a large drum for the lower sound and near the rim for the higher one. Substitute other sound sources if large drums are not available.)

Have the students:

- Practice the pattern without instruments.

  (They should use their dominant hand as the playing hand, holding their non-dominant hand at about waist level. Have them pat the lower notes and clap the higher notes, saying "low" and "high" as they pat and clap.)

Students will learn the pattern more easily if they are guided to discover the following:

  a. The lower notes are always played two in groups of two.
  b. The pattern of the upper notes is 3-1-3.
  c. The first five sounds (L-L-H-H-H) and the last
       five are identical, separated only by L-L-H in the middle.

- Listen to *Under the Sun* again, doing the pattern when it occurs (From 0:20 to 2:00 and from 4:40 to 5:27, the end.). (Repeat, taking turns on available drums.)
- Listen to *On the Steppes of Central Asia*, by Alexander Borodin, to compare *Under the Sun* with a different composer's musical description of vast stretches of arid land.
- Improvise their own music describing the desert on recorders, or other pitched instruments, while some students play the drum pattern. Use long, sustained, non-metric rhythms on the pitched instruments to create the feeling of the vastness of the open desert. (**Student page #25**)

PAUL WINTER'S THOUGHTS ON IMPROVISATION:

Each of us has a natural instinct for spontaneous response that we have used in conversation all our speaking lives. In music, that same ability, easily applied to producing spontaneous sounds with instruments or voices, is improvisation. Improvising is one of the great keys to expression.

In a small group context, simultaneous improvisation enables each player to participate in a shared journey that results in a living tapestry of melodic threads, full of surprise and spontaneous energy. It is this process of collectively 'growing' original pieces that the Paul Winter Consort has used for many years in creating its music.

Free collaborative improvisation leads into the realm of 'not-knowing,' being guided by your ears, awakening your instincts. This state is akin to that of 'wildness' in animals - that quality of aliveness to their environment which wild creatures must have at all times if they are to survive. We humans sometimes refer to a state of heightened awareness as a 'peak experience' - a label which implies how infrequently we know this condition of full-aliveness. In music-making it is possible to reach this state quickly and sustain it. This opens up possibilities for a way of life that is transformed by music-making.

FINAL EXPERIENCE: Have the students combine their spoken and musical descriptions as an introduction, then move to the recording and/or their own improvisations.

Name _____ Date _____

Student Page #23 *Map of the World*

Directions: Fill in each rectangle, correctly labeling the geographic area to which each is related. Research and label several principal desert areas of the world. Work alone, or in small groups, as directed by the teacher.

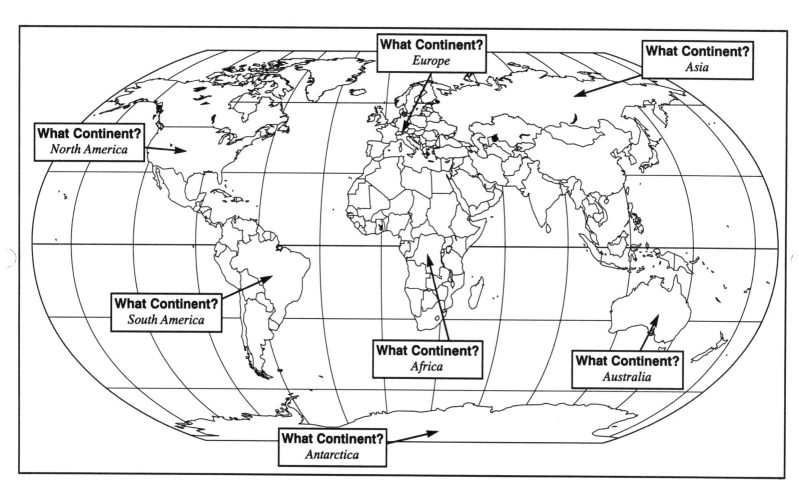

Student Page #24: *Under the Sun*

Directions:

1. Read the following description of the composition, *Under the Sun*.

> *Pulse of the desert drum, beat of the earth;*
> > *the day's vibrations hum in expectancy the final chord.*
> *The sun, sinking, bursts in its evening ritual of consecration.*
> *Melt-colors of amber, orange, rose, red and purple,*
> > *as one wave, washes over the horizon rim, a life-giving, unifying flood.*
> *Then the tide subsides:*
> > *earth drains the sky, drinks in the colors and the fire.*
> *Dusk brings its own whispering beauty.*

2. Listen to *Under the Sun* again, with attention to the instruments used this time. List here any you can identify. After the music is over, compare your answers with others in the class, and with the teacher's answers.

3. Write here any features of the music that you notice and a brief description of how the music changes as it goes along. What do you think the changes in the music might represent?

4. In the space below, reflect on how the different stages of a desert sunset might look, then write your own description of the different stages of sunset on the desert . Try to make your description about four sentences or phrases long.

Student Page #25: *A Desert Sun Improvisation*

Directions:

1. Learn to play the following pattern on drums. Then, play it with *Under the Sun*.
   The drum pattern requires two different pitches played on a single drum. This is done by playing in the middle of a large drum for the lower sound and near the rim for the higher one. Substitute other sound sources if large drums are not available.

2. In small groups, take turns improvising your own melodies describing the desert. Use recorders or other pitched instruments for the melody, while some students play the drum pattern. Use long, sustained, non-metric rhythms (rhythms without a definite beat or pattern) on the pitched instruments to create the feeling of the vastness of the open desert and to provide contrast to the strict rhythm of the drum pattern. Begin softly, then slowly *crescendo* (gradually get louder*)* and *decrescendo* (gradually get softer). Fade out to silence at the end. Before you begin, you may need to decide who will play each instrument and how you will know when one person is to turn the role of improvisor over to another. Use the space below to plan your improvisation.

Names of improvisors in your group:

_____

_____

Names of drummers in your group:

_____

_____

Method of changing from one improvisor to another:

Pre-planned Number of Seconds Per Improvisor?   Yes _____   No _____

Conductor Indicates Change of Improvisor?   Yes _____   No _____

Other method ? (Please explain briefly here.)

12. AND THE EARTH SPINS (FINALE)
by Paul Halley/Back Alley Music, ASCAP

Outcome Choices:
1. Brief written descriptions of the important new insights they have gained from these lessons and how it will affect them and their future attitudes and actions.
2. A presentation of some of the creative work from the class, based on one of the musical selections. (These could be shared with the other classes that have been involved and/or with the rest of the school as a final experience for this project.)

The First Hearing

Before:
• Have the students listen as you (or a student) read the essays they may have written.

During:
• Have the students listen to the music, thinking of what they have learned about taking care of the Earth and its inhabitants in this series of lessons.

After:
• Have a few students take turns telling some of the things they thought of during the music. Have them continue their discussions in small groups and write down, then share, their answers with the class.

Getting to Know the Music

Have the students:
• Listen again, to identify any instruments they can.
  (Instruments used: soprano saxophone, flute, cello, keyboards, bass, drums, steel-string guitar, and Heckelphone. The Heckelphone is in the oboe family, but plays an octave lower. It has a wide conical bore and a rounded bell. It was invented in 1904 by Wilhelm Heckel but has never been widely used in spite of its full, rich sound.)
• Become more familiar with the music by watching the following outline on the board, or on **Student page 26:** *Listening to **And The Earth Spins**,* as they listen to identify each section.

1 - A	(0:00)	Main theme (long, sustained, hymn-like)	
2 - B	(0:55)	Second theme (shorter sounds, more active)	
3 - A	(1:24)	Main theme (flute)	
4 - B	(1:36)	Second theme (saxophone enters during this part)	
5 - C	(1:55)	Third theme (saxophone)	
6 - A	(2:23)	Main Theme	
7 - B	(2:39)	Second theme (piano prominent)	
8 - C	(3:10)	Third theme (saxophone)	
9 - C	(3:37)	Third theme in new key (saxophone)	
10 - A	(4:07)	Main theme, more extended (all play)	
11 - CODA	(4:45)		

(TOTAL TIME - 5:06)

Have the students reflect on, then write, a brief description of one of the important new insights they have gained from these lessons and how it will affect them and their future attitudes and actions. Suggestion: You may wish to have them discuss this in small groups, then either write individually or as a small group effort.

Musical Discoveries

Practice the 3/4 Meter

Have the students

- Listen to the music, moving on the downbeat in 3/4 meter.
- Form three groups to represent themes A, B, or C. Each group decides on a different formation and a different way to move on the downbeat.
- Move at their designated times as they listen again, showing the form through movement.

FINAL EXPERIENCE: *EARTH — VOICES OF A PLANET*

As a final experience for this entire project, consider having several classes meet together, each presenting some of its creative work that has been based on one of the musical selections. These could be shared with the other classes that have been involved and/or with the rest of the school.

See the FINAL EXPERIENCE paragraph at the end of the suggestions for each selection for specific ideas.

For a beginning and an ending, you may wish to have all the participants sing *Garden of the Earth*.

Each class could represent one continent, or one of the important features of the earth (ocean, mountains, desert).

For the final selection, *And the Earth Spins*, one class, or representatives from each class, could present a dance in which nine solo dancers or small groups would each represent one continent, or geographical feature (desert, oceans, mountains). One person or group, costumed appropriately — or wearing symbols or other labels to show what they represent, could enter at the beginning of each of the first nine sections.

On the final appearance of the main theme (Section 10. See outline.) they could move into a circle formation, and walk in the circle while stepping on the downbeat, in the style of a processional. As the composition ends, all could turn out and raise their hands skyward. (If a double circle is needed, those in the outer ring could kneel down so that those in the inner ring would be more visible.)

The program could then end with all participants, and the audience, joining hands and singing *Garden of the Earth*. (See page 89 for Orff instrument orchestration and **Student page #27** for music manuscript). The words can be put in a program, or on a transparency for the audience to see.

Student Page #26: *Listening to And The Earth Spins*

Directions: Follow the outline below as you listen to the music. This will help you to become familiar with the music. Think of how the music represents the spinning of the earth. Think of how the music might be used as part of a performance for others about taking care of our Earth and all its voices.

1	-	A	(0:00)	Main theme (long, sustained, hymn - like)
2	-	B	(0:55)	Second theme (shorter sounds, more active)
3	-	A	(1:24)	Main theme (flute)
4	-	B	(1:36)	Second theme (saxophone enters during this part)
5	-	C	(1:55)	Third theme (saxophone)
6	-	A	(2:23)	Main Theme
7	-	B	(2:39)	Second theme (piano prominent)
8	-	C	(3:10)	Third theme (saxophone)
9	-	C	(3:37)	Third theme in new key (saxophone)
10	-	A	(4:07)	Main theme, more extended (all play)
11	-	CODA	(4:45)	

(TOTAL TIME - 5:06)

Name_____Date _____

Student Page #27: *Garden of the Earth*
(Recorded on *Earthbeat,* by Paul Winter.)

Traditional Russian Folk Song
Words by Paul Winter and Paul Halley
Arranged by Dr. ROBERT DeFRECE, 1993

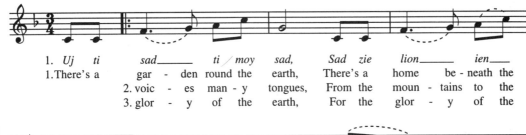

1. *Uj ti sad_____ ti / moy sad, Sad zie lion_____ ien_____*
1. There's a gar - den round the earth, There's a home be - neath the
2. voic - es man - y tongues, From the moun - tains to the
3. glor - y of the earth, For the glor - y of the

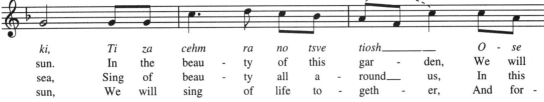

ki, Ti za cehm ra no tsve tiosh_____ O - se
sun. In the beau - ty of this gar - den, We will
sea, Sing of beau - ty all a - round__ us, In this
sun, We will sing of life to - geth - er, And for -

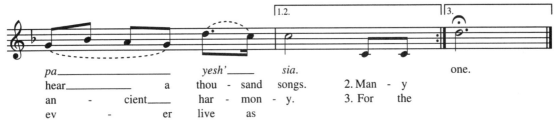

pa_____ yesh'____ sia. one.
hear_____ a thou - sand songs. 2. Man - y
an - cient___ har - mon - y. 3. For the
ev - er live as

FOR

The Rt. index finger touches the forehead and then moves outward.

GLORY

The fluttering middle fingers describe two opposing arcs in the air.

EARTH

The Rt. thumb and middle finger move back and forth on the top of the L.H.

SUN
The index finger describes a circle above the head. The closed fingertip hand moves down and opens, ie. rays shining down.

SING
Place the closed fingertips at the corners of the mouth and move hands forward in a gesture of singing.

LIFE/LIVE

Use this sign for both "life"and "live". Both hands in "L" position and palms facing in, move up the body.

TOGETHER

Both hands touch in "A" position. Palms facing each other.

FOREVER
The upright finger describes a small circle, palm facing in, then moves to a "Y" palm out, away from the body.

AS

Both index fingers pointing forward, touch side to side with palms down.

ONE (United)

The index and thumbs are hooked with other fingers extended. Move the hands in a large circle, right, forward, left.

GARDEN OF THE EARTH

RUSSIAN FOLK SONG
Words by Paul Winter and Paul Halley
Arranged by Dr. ROBERT DeFRECE 1993

PROCESS:

1. Learn melody and words.
2. Present recorder parts on visual charts.
3. Use the following visual to teach voice parts in the last verse:
   3.1 Have the children sing the numbers, moving up and down one scale step from the designated pitch.
   3.2 When the children can successfully perform their parts together with the numbers, have them change to "Ah" and the words shown in parentheses.
4. Teach the children the signs for the last verse.
5. The pitched-percussion parts can be learned from visuals of notation. The transposition up one tone for the last verse is optional–you could choose to remain in F-major, but the key-change is certainly in the style of the song.
6. A piano accompaniment using the chord symbols shown maintains the forward motion of the melody line.

This song would be a good choice for an Earth Day Celebration.

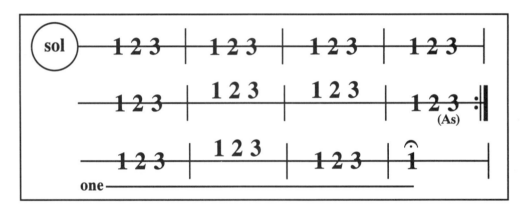

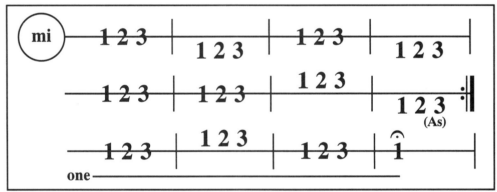

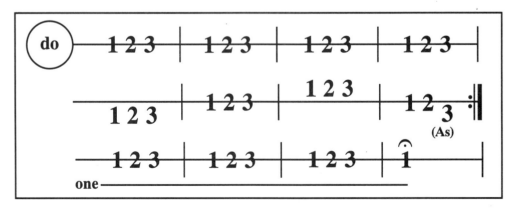

The Music of
PAUL WINTER

EARTH: VOICES OF A PLANET
by Marilyn Copeland Davidson

PROJECT RECORDS/PLANNER

1. Appalachian Morning				
2. Cathedral Forest				
3. Call of the Elephant				
4. Antarctica				
5. Ocean Child				
6. Uirapurú Do Amazonas				
7. Talkabout				
8. Russian Girls				
9. Black Forest				
10. Song of the Exile				
11. Under the Sun				
12. And the Earth Spins				

Other titles by Paul Winter and Friends available from Living Music include:

Prayer for the Wild Things . . . . LMUS 0028

Spanish Angel . . . . LMUS 0027

*Solstice Live! . . . . LMUS 0024

Songs of the Humpback Whale . . . . . . LMUS 0021

Wolf Eyes . . . . LMUS 0018

Earthbeat . . . . LMUS 0013

Whales Alive! . . . . LMUS 0013

Wintersong . . . . LMUS 0012

Canyon . . . . LMUS 0006

Sun Singer . . . . LMUS 0003

Missa Gaia/Earth Mass . . . . LMUS 0002

Calling . . . . LMUS 0001

Living Music, P.O. Box 72B, Litchfield, CT 06759
1-800-437-2281

*Teacher's Guide by Marilyn Davidson available in the fall of 1995